THE CRITICS

Mad About Macarons! by Jill Colonna is lavishly photographed with lots of clear steps of the process of how to make classic macarons as well as interesting and unusual variations (curry, chocolate-beet, and pistachio-wasabi to name a few). If you like macarons, it's likely you'll love this book.

David Lebovitz

This book will appeal to travel and food readers as well as bakers. Scottish-born Colonna writes extensively about her experience moving to France and searching for her place amid its culture, language, and cuisine … By revealing her own early uncertainties and ultimate successes, she makes macaron recipes approachable for apprehensive bakers.

The US Library Journal

The author provides detailed and precise steps for readers looking to tackle everything from traditional flavors, like Chocolate-Hazelnut, to more unusual and exhilarating combinations like Pistachio-White Chocolate-Wasabi or Prune-Armagnac-Orange … Suggested wine and tea pairings for each recipe are also a nice touch, as are the author's suggestions for how to use all those pesky egg yolks you've discarded when creating your egg-white-only macaron masterpieces.

Kirkus Reviews, "The World's Toughest Book Critics"

When your visit to Paris is a distant memory and the taste of macarons has long since faded from your tongue, you can recreate the magic at home with Jill's book. Play it safe with traditional rose flavour, or walk on the wild side with Bloody Mary macs or Thai Green Curry. Just don't tell Mr Hermé or the good people at Ladurée.

Mel Fenson, ParisVoice Webzine

Masterchef-junkies bewildered by all that messing about with macaroons in the last series – les macarons having replaced the cupcake as the must-have dessert de nos jours – can learn how to do it right in Jill Colonna's ***Mad about Macarons!***

Elizabeth Luard, The Scotsman

THE FOOD BLOGGERS

A work of meringue-sandwiched brilliance. Jill is the Martha Stewart of macaronnage.

ParisPâtisseries

Mad About Macarons! is my go-to delicious guide for making macarons.

ParisBreakfasts

The only book you'll need on macarons. It covers everything you need to know in a beautiful and clear way.

Manu's Menu

They turned out absolutely perfect, with much higher feet than I've ever gotten! Thank you so much for restoring my confidence with macarons.

EatandBeHappy

Now I know how easy these gems are, I'll be dreaming up my next batches. If you'd like to make your own macarons ... please buy your own copy of ***Mad About Macarons*** ... or borrow mine, but not for long!

That Skinny Chick Can Bake!

Thank you so much for writing a great book that really makes creating macarons at home *si facile*!

The Culinary Librarian

Jill's recipe is pretty perfect ... the ratio of ground almonds to powdered sugar in her recipe compared to others really made a difference.

Sweets by Sillianah

If you love macarons or desserts in general, for sure you will enjoy Jill's gorgeous and delicious works of art.

Just One Cookbook

Every recipe I have tried has been perfect ... the book is fantastic.

The Art of Being Perfect

This is one of the most comprehensive cookbooks that I've bought in a long time (and I buy a lorra cookbooks).

A Village Pantry

THE CUSTOMERS
(FROM AMAZON.COM AND AMAZON.CO.UK)

This is by far the best macaron book yet ... makes making macarons a piece of cake.

I am a pastry chef and I can say that this is the best macaron book out there.

My first batch came out PERFECT!! This book is the reason why!

Just finished my first batch from the book, they turned out perfect!

It takes the frustration out of trying to make macarons. No more flubbed shells with this method!

My Macaron Holy Book: I own three cookbooks dedicated to the *Macaron Parisien* and this is by far the best of any I have read.

A faultless basic recipe that is easy to follow.

The only macaron book you will ever need. I have produced batch after batch of delicious macarons.

Absolutely foolproof!... My first attempt was a total success – they looked and tasted great.

Mad about Macarons!

To Antoine,

Julie and Lucie

For bonus recipes, Le Blog, tips and Jill's news go to
MadAboutMacarons.com

Join in the fun with the Mad About Macarons! community on
Facebook.com/MadAboutMacarons

Mad about Macarons!

Jill Colonna

WAVERLEY
BOOKS

Acknowledgements:
Un grand merci *to my dear family and friends who have patiently endured my mad macaron world.*

With special thanks to Emeric Lemoine and Belinda Hopkinson for their advice and support; to Ron Grosset, Liz Small, Kenny Allan, Mark Mechan and Eleanor Abraham for their dynamic enthusiasm; and to Julie and Lucie: for being uncomplaining during photos when Mum's macarons are just-for-looking-at, being inspiring macaron tasters and, along with my husband, Antoine, providing endless encouragement.

Now I invite all 'macaronivores' *to enjoy them, too.* Enfin*!*

First published 2010 by Waverley Books, 144 Port Dundas Road, Glasgow G4 0HZ, Scotland.
Reprinted 2010, 2011 (three times)

Other elements, backgrounds, decoration courtesy of Shutterstock: p.1, 2-3 LadyAnn; p.8 Junker; p.8, 32, 50, 66, 94 ElenaShow; flourishes p.3 and throughout book Sanjar; p.32, 106 Aneta Witkowska; p.32 Lady_Diana; p. 32 candycatdesigns; p.44 Elena Itsenko; p.50, 66, 120 Studio DMM Photography, Designs & Art; p.94 Nina Malyna; p.101 Michael Hansen; p.115 Yuri Arcurs.

Layout design consultants El Studio, www.el-studio.co.uk

A catalogue entry for this book is available from the British Library.

978-1-84934-041-0

Printed and bound in Indonesia.

Typeset in Bitstream Typo Upright, Bauer Bodoni and Humanist.

MadAboutMacarons.com

CONTENTS

Introduction

Plain But Fancy

Chocolate Combinations

Create a Storm with Your Teacup

Mad Macs

Dazzling Macaron Desserts

Appendix

INTRODUCTION

I dare you to try not to become mad about macarons – eating and making them.

Once you try to make them you'll be hooked. They taste delicious and they look incredibly stylish. Your friends cannot fail to be impressed. Give them as delightful gifts, party or wedding favours or surprise your dinner party guests with mini savoury macaron *apéritifs* before a meal, or sweet macaron *mignardises* at the end.

Think macarons are hard to make?

This colourful and delicious pâtisserie has the reputation of being devilishly difficult to make and accordingly it has a price tag to match.

But you ***can*** make them at home. Forget the recipes that suggest you stack two baking trays on top of each other, rap the tray on the table or change the temperature midway through. There's even no need for a pâtisserie thermometer since we're making French meringue, not Italian.

If you follow the basic recipe in *Mad About Macarons* to the letter you'll have picture-perfect macarons.

Mad about Macarons!

A LITTLE TASTE OF PARIS

Brightly coloured Parisian macarons are so temptingly dressed here in France with highly imaginative displays in pâtisserie windows. But at a less tempting price per kilo, it's motivation enough to create them at home yourself.

After some experimentation and endless tasting sessions, I have reduced the sugar content as much as can be dared without affecting the macaron's appearance. Several of the recipes are inspired by the great pâtisserie masters of macarons, but are simplified to make our lives at home easier. Others I have concocted myself, using the basic recipe outlined on pages 24–29 and some more unusual ingredients!

So that those with nut allergies needn't miss out, I've invented the nut-free macaron (see page 48), made with delicious nutty-tasting quinoa. My children – my fiercest critics – said they were delicious.

I'm particularly proud of my spicy concoctions. The combination of fiery spices with the sweet macaron is absolutely dynamite. Tikka Macsala, Beetroot and Horseradish or Thai Green Curry (see pages 100, 103 and 105) can also be served as *amuse-bouches* or unique *entrées* to surprise your guests.

The basic recipe outlined in this book requires precise measuring and careful following of instructions but it's not difficult. You'll discover that it's also easy to make pastry cream or chocolate ganache fillings. Once you've mastered the classic flavours of macarons you can then go on to produce more adventurous varieties.

I've added tips to give the macarons a professional look, too. Dress them to impress as flowers in a flowerpot (see page 93) or create your own chocolate dome for special occasions (see page 90). In addition, you can transform macarons into dazzling desserts. Without much effort, you can produce giant macarons topped with lightly perfumed cream and seasonal fruits.

AMERICAN READERS

You might be disappointed not to see measurements in cups. We're not forgetting you. It's just that, in my experience, cups are not an accurate enough measurement to enable you to make macarons consistently well. I recommend that all readers measure in grammes and buy digital scales to ensure that your measuring is as precise as it needs to be. Also, if any British cookery terms are puzzling there's a list on page 128 to help you.

Argentine
Porte
Dauphine
6
Charles
de Gaulle
Étoile
George V
Kléber
Franklin

What is a Parisian "Macaron"?

IS IT A COCONUT CAKE OR A MERINGUE?

When I first heard of the macaroon, it was the macaroon bar from Scotland with its fondant centre and topping of chocolate and shredded coconut. The word macaroon can refer to two varieties of biscuits that are either meringue-based or made of coconut.

Macaroons date back to the Renaissance, and by the 18th century they resembled the Italian-style amaretti biscuit. It was in the early 20th century, however, that the modern *macaron* from Paris was introduced.

In the picture opposite you'll see two sandwich cookies. The one on the left with its rough surface and pointy top is made from two nutty Italian amaretti biscuits sandwiched together.

The one on the right has a smooth surface, a little frilly foot or *pied*, a crispy outside and a soft, light filling. That's the Parisian macaron. If a cookie does not have the ruffled pied it's not a macaron.

What we're referring to in this book is known as the *gerbet* or Parisian macaron (pronounced ma-kah-ron). It's a meringue-based confection with two outer crispy shells sandwiched together with a soft filling. It was created in the early 20th century by Pierre Desfontaines. He was the second cousin of Louis Ernest Ladurée, founder of the celebrated macaron pâtisserie, *Ladurée*.

The French macaron, according to *Larousse Gastronomique*, comes from the Italian *maccherone,* or Venetian *macarone*, meaning finely crushed or a fine paste. The paste consists of the ground almonds, egg whites and sugar that form the macaron's characteristic silky smooth dome and its ruffled and airy base.

So that there is no confusion, let's keep the word macaroon for other coconut and almond sandwich biscuit varieties and *macaron* for the meringue-based confection.

Macarons are simple to make at home. It just requires a certain technique to get it right. This book will help you to uncover the secrets of this adorable French pâtisserie.

Make Macarons like the French

SO YOU'RE MAD ABOUT PARISIAN MACARONS?

So you're mad about macarons? That makes two of us – and the majority of the French gourmet population. If you are not familiar with them yet, well be prepared: they will hook you too. They are the luxuries of the gastronomic world. It's amazing how these delicate pâtisseries have a growing following. Look on the internet and you'll be amazed at the number of fan clubs and associations there are for enthusiasts to compare views on the latest *parfums* or flavours to be unveiled in fashionable *maisons de pâtisseries* in Paris and elsewhere – whether it be London, Geneva, Sydney, New York, Shanghai or Tokyo. Luxury jewellers have been inspired by macarons to produce rock-studded works of art in the shape of the stylish little cake. On March 20th, the French even celebrate the *Fête du Macaron* with the arrival of spring.

Macarons are to the French food-lover's world what cupcakes are to the rest. But, while cupcakes have to be eaten relatively quickly in order to retain their freshly moist texture, macarons cannot even be eaten for the first 24 hours. Just ask my children – they couldn't wait to eat them when they were fresh but dry and then they tasted them the next day when the centre had moistened into the meringue. They confirmed there was no comparison and are now so patient to savour them properly and just ***wait***. The next day they are perfect. They will keep in the fridge for up to a week and still be absolutely sensational. The outer crust remains light and crispy whilst the fragrant creamy centre penetrates into the meringue to make the middle of the macaron soft, intriguing and decadent. What's more, they are **gluten free**.

WARNING! MACARONS CAN BECOME ADDICTIVE TO MAKE!

A childlike rush of excitement can take hold just watching these little meringue domes rise in the oven, forming beautiful airy "feet" at the bottom. The greatest satisfaction is seeing family and friends admire them, followed by that long expectant first bite. In true gourmet style, these are not gobbled but *dégustés* (tasted). You'll see. Create your own macaron concoctions based on the following recipes. Just put aside those egg whites, allow your creativity to take over and watch everyone around you become entranced.

And, unlike cupcakes, macarons taste even better the next day and the next … and the next …

Discovering the Macaron

AND DISCOVERING I COULD MAKE MY OWN

When I came to live in France nearly 20 years ago I didn't have a sweet tooth. Dessert was just an apple and some cheese. But the beckoning Parisian pâtisseries had me quickly lured in by their sophisticated window displays and I was converted. How can you resist a perfectly presented delicacy called *un mille feuille* (a thousand leaves), crammed with fragrant vanilla custard cream between flaky, toasted layers of pastry under an artistic icing?

Suddenly I felt so far away from our local baker in Edinburgh who produced something similar, but called it a *mayo fayo* with a posh accent. I wanted to practise this new mouthful, repeating "un mille feuille, s'il vous plaît" in so many pâtisseries until I discovered the best cakes in our Parisian *arrondissement* and until I was no longer snootily corrected for my atrocious French accent. There was so much to learn.

After tasting my way through the pâtisserie classics using my student lunch money, it was finally a relief to be a working girl, working in Paris, in a château, in a chic part of town.

Occasionally I could indulge in the opulence of a *salon de thé* (tea salon), drinking tea from a porcelain cup. It was fascinating: like having afternoon tea in a grand hotel's palm court but without the piano or the sandwiches. The women were so stylish and slim! French women don't eat between meals. They are so strict at sticking to mealtimes. I had a friend who if she missed lunch was so disciplined that she would not eat until her tea and gâteau at 4 o'clock. They eat well and they stay slim.

Ten years ago, macarons were not in most pâtisseries as they are now in Paris. It was in Paris that I discovered the macaron. It was during a lunch break with the girls at the salon de thé on the top floor of a seriously classy ladies' department store in the 16th arrondissement. The macaron was on all the elegant ladies' plates like a fashion accessory.

It was love at first sight: they were perfection on a porcelain plate, so airy and delicate that you didn't feel like you'd have to play at dress sizes if you became hooked, yet they were just big enough to savour and appreciate their sweet voluptuous perfumed centre with a refreshing cuppa.

They looked so perfect and dainty and certainly not something you could obviously make at home. That was for the professionals, I thought.

The move to France was initially tough, coping with the language and adjusting to the culture. Their entertainment was inviting each other around for dinner, rather than going out. The conversation flowed, the wine flowed and my French apparently flowed better with the wine (I had a diploma in wine so had an excuse). As a real chatterbox, it was frustrating for me to carefully construct a phrase to join in the discussion with my husband's friends at the dinner table, only to find by the time I was ready to contribute, the conversation had moved on and I looked like the daft Scottish lass. My pride was at stake. I had to impress them on a plate.

My husband's present one Christmas was a cookery course in Paris. It confirmed many things I was doing already and so it surprisingly boosted my confidence in the kitchen. I adore French restaurants. We do the French thing and entertain at home, so when we do go out occasionally, they are *gastronomique* affairs: from hidden Parisian bistros to sophisticated starred tables. That's where I can be inspired.

One day I saw a local pâtisserie holding a macaron workshop and I went for it. In the space of a couple of hours I was shown the tricks of the trade and suddenly realised that it was so much easier than it looked. Later, I experimented at home with different flavours, eliminating jam fillings to cut down on sugar. I would get up some mornings thinking, "The egg whites are ready! What flavours shall I try?" [It is best to age egg whites for at least four days when making macarons.] The biggest thrill was watching those around me look so impressed by the results. I could make macarons and I'm not even French!

My confidence also improved with speaking the language. My bi-lingual children correct me too, which is so comforting. I often dream in French – and I dream about making macarons with my children: their favourite job is not only tasting them but also marrying up the pairs before putting on their glorious fillings.

I'm now a *macaronivore*. My children are my best critics and so are interrogated with questions such as "Is that the right colour for a beetroot macaron?" and "Is this curry macaron too spicy?"

You may also be cast under the spell of macaron-making madness, of which I take absolutely no responsibility. Just give it a go: be imaginative, creative and you will impress friends and family with the most gratifying, do-it-yourself, glamorous and state-of-the art confection: the macaron!

Storing Macarons

THAT IS, IF YOU CAN BEAR NOT TO EAT THEM ALL!

Macarons can keep for up to a week if kept chilled in the fridge. I use a number of different containers to store them: such as lidded plastic fruit packaging saved from the supermarket. The mini ones fit perfectly into long cherry-tomato boxes.

Sealed plastic containers work well, as do biscuit tins. My favourite, however, are actual carton cake boxes, below, which I use when giving macarons as presents.

Macarons can also freeze well for up to three months. Simply defrost them an hour before serving them at room temperature. By freezing them in advance, you can always impress guests as you magically produce a whole variety of flavours on the same presentation plate!

Remember to take macarons out of the fridge at least 30 minutes before tasting them to appreciate their full flavour. Chocolate macarons need to be out of the fridge for one hour.

Great Mac Gifts

CHIC BOXES, BAGS AND RIBBONS

Macarons make great gifts. Ideal for that simple but luxurious "thank you". For a small presentation of about six macarons, I use clear cellophane bags (see Stockists, page 127) and keep a bag of ribbons saved from previous wrappings to recycle for little gift packs. I buy large giftwrapping ribbons for the larger cake boxes.

For bigger gift boxes, you can buy carton cake boxes from speciality cake shops or online (see Stockists) to make your home-made macarons look as if they've come directly from a terribly chic French pâtisserie!

Add an Extra Touch of Class

BE CREATIVE

Once the macarons are cooked it's so simple to finish them off with a quick dusting of **chocolate powder** or **icing sugar** using a chocolate duster. For a shiny gold, silver or bronzed look, dust the tops of the macarons with edible culinary **metallic colouring** (or **edible lustre**, for Stockists see page 127). Brush, dust or rub it on, gently coating the top half with your fingertip.

Create a tartan effect or make spirals with **melted chocolate**: use a small writing piping bag with a mini nozzle. Simply dollop a tiny bit of melted chocolate on the macaron tops using the back of a spoon. Or be artistic by brushing on melted chocolate with a pastry brush.

Before cooking and before the macarons set, at *croûter* stage (see page 28), you can **decorate** with crushed nuts, or other sprinkles that will not melt in the oven.

Also at *croûter* stage, for a **spray of vivid colour**, dip a fine paintbrush in liquid colouring and simply spray it onto the shells by tapping the brush with your fingers (see page 78).

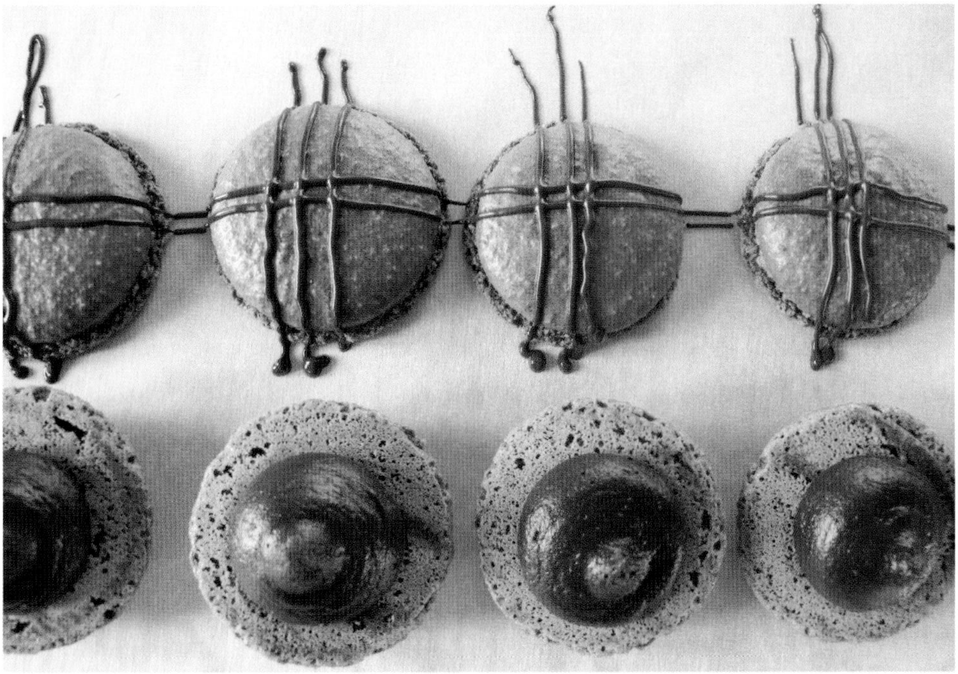

Weddings

BE A LITTLE DIFFERENT

Boxes or bags containing one or two macarons are becoming very fashionable to give as **wedding favours**. (For Stockists see page 127.) Create shiny macarons and rub on some metallic lustre. Serve platters of them in the middle of each table: almond macarons with silver or lilac dusting, rose with metallic pink lustre, vanilla with gold, and bronzed chocolate. They will all look stunning to complement after-dinner coffee on your special day.

Alternatively, use a macaron shell for place names. As there is no need for any ganache fillings, they can be prepared in advance and stored in airtight jars up to a week before the big day. Colour them to match your wedding theme – or use pink for the girls, lilac for the boys – brushing on some lustre before adding guests' names using writing icing or with pens that have liquid food colour as ink (see Stockists).

Macarons are quite fragile so bear this in mind when planning to serve them at weddings. Keep it simple. Because they freeze so well you can prepare them a few weeks in advance. You could freeze the shells then make the fillings and assemble the macarons one or two days before the big event, or freeze them complete with fillings, already in their gift bags or boxes. You're going to need plenty of freezer and fridge space so be prepared. Don't take on the job if you don't have adeqate space to store them. Bag or box them up carefully and leave adequate space around them so that they do not crack or get crushed. Check that they are intact a week before the event so that there is time to make more if any have become damaged.

If you are the bride, give someone else the job of carefully transporting them to your event on the day!

Make a few more than you need in case of inevitable breakages or inadvertent misspellings.

Don't attempt anything you haven't tried a few times before. For example, you'll see elaborate conical towers of macarons at some weddings – difficult for the amateur cook to achieve. You can't be sure of the temperature of the room in your venue and so the "glue" you use (such as chocolate or caramel) may melt. Someone will have to construct it right there at the venue. If you are the bride – or even a key guest of the bride – this might all be too much to achieve on the day of the wedding without a lot of stress and worry.

Antoine
Ron
Lucie
David

Julie

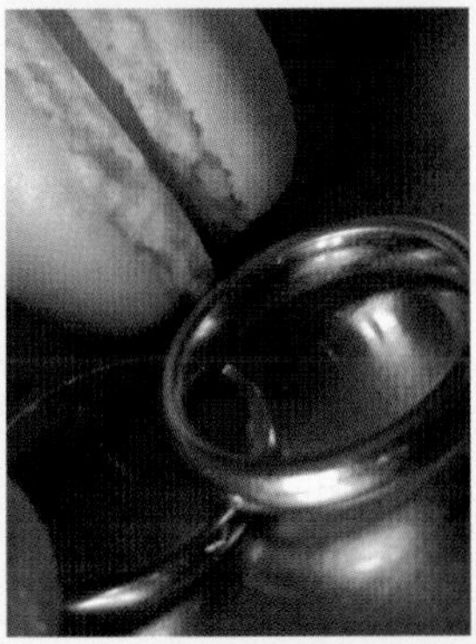

Macarons: The Basic Recipe

MINI, MEDIUM OR GIANT MACARONS

Ingredients:

150g organic egg whites, aged for 4 to 5 days (see Egg Tips on opposite page)
100g fine caster sugar (superfine sugar)
180g ground almonds (almond flour)
270g icing sugar (10X or confectioner's sugar)

Makes approximately:
60 mini macarons or
40 medium-sized macarons or
15 giant macarons

They take approximately
2 hours to make:—
30 minutes preparation,
30 minutes resting,
12 minutes cooking,
45 minutes assembly.

Equipment:

1 Electronic digital scales are essential. Measurements must be exact.
2 A hand-held or stand-alone electric whisk (and also a hand whisk for the fillings).
3 A large spatula (flexible, either rubber or silicone).
4 A 40-cm (16") piping bag (either disposable or a good nylon or silicone washable bag).
5 A plain nozzle for the piping bag (8–10mm [¾–½"]).
6 A flexible plastic pâtisserie scraper. The scraper will also enable you to easily push out all the mixture in the piping bag.
7 Three flat baking sheets (sheetpans) lined with baking parchment.
8 A medium sieve.
9 Two mixing bowls.

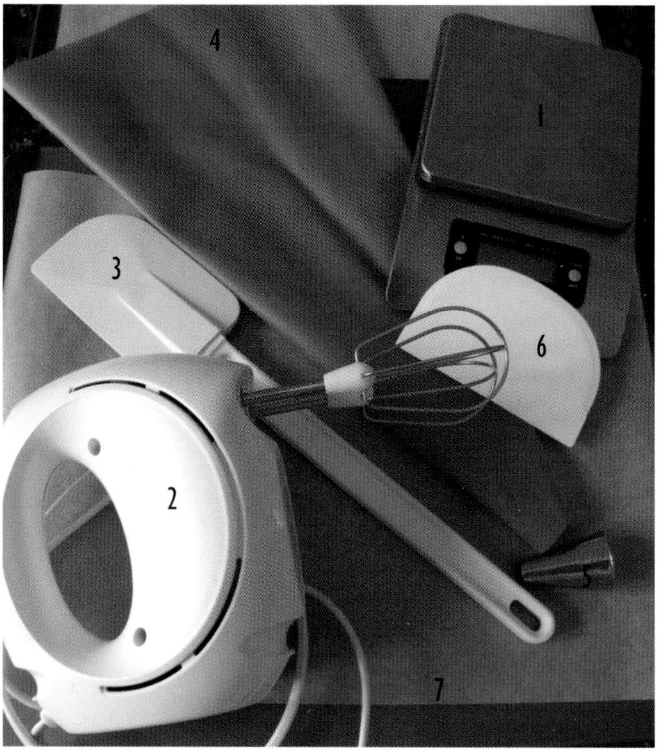

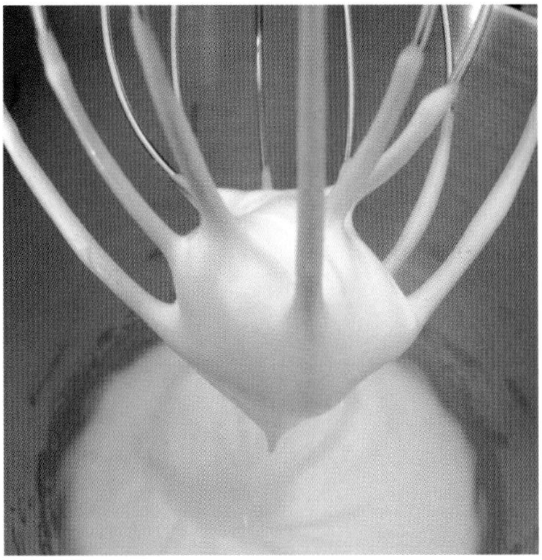

1 Line your three flat baking sheets with perfectly flat baking parchment and set aside.

2 Whisk the egg whites (at room temperature) to glossy firm peaks, adding the caster sugar gradually. (Tip: ensure the bowl and whisk are perfectly clean. Any trace of fat, yolk or soap will affect the success.)
If making coloured macarons, then add a dash of colouring (I prefer to use powdered colours or pastes, as less is needed) towards the end of mixing.

EGG TIPS

* To easily separate egg whites from yolks: crack the egg in the middle on the edge of a bowl or another hard surface. With clean hands, over a bowl, gently drop the egg into the palm of one hand, letting the white drip through your fingers into the bowl, leaving the yolk in the palm of your hand.
No need to waste the yolks: see page 121.

* When making macarons (or meringues) you get the best results from egg whites that have been separated and aged for four to five days in the refrigerator. For 150g of egg white you'll need approximately 5 eggs. Store in a perfectly clean airtight container such as a glass jar.
Take them out of the fridge 2 hours before use to bring to room temperature.

3 Sift the ground almonds with the icing sugar using a medium sieve. Discard any large, coarse pieces of ground almonds.
(Tip: if there are a lot of large pieces to discard, weigh them and replace them in the mixture with more ground almonds to make sure you still have the 180g specified.)

For chocolate macarons (as I am making here) also sift in the 10g of cocoa at this point.

4 Mix well to incorporate icing sugar and almonds (and cocoa powder if you are using it).

5 Incorporate the beaten egg whites into the dry ingredients using a large spatula. Mix well.

(Note that there is no need to "fold" the mixture.)

6 Then work on the mixture (*macaronnage*) using a plastic scraper (*corne en plastique*). Press down well with the scraper, going back and forward, to press out the oxygen from the whites. Do this for no more than 5 minutes until you have a smooth mixture.

(It helps if your bowl is flat in the middle.)

7 The result should form a soft and brilliant mixture that forms a "ribbon" on the scraper.

If the mixture is too liquid, through too much macaronnage, the macarons may be flat, crack or have no *pieds*.

If the mixture is too thick, through insufficient macaronnage, the macarons may have little points on the surface after piping.

8 Transfer the mixture to a piping bag with a plain nozzle (approx. 1cm [½"]) round the tip). Twist or clip the bag above the nozzle to stop the mixture escaping.

You'll find it easier if you turn down the top of the bag before putting in the mixture with the spatula. That way you can unfold the bag at the top when the mixture is in and you won't have a mess around the top of the bag or on your work surface.

PIPING BAG

* Supporting your piping bag in a tall jug or a pint glass can make it easier to fill the bag. (Twist or clip the bag above the nozzle.)

* You can use the scraper to push out all the macaron mixture or filling to the tip of the piping bag.

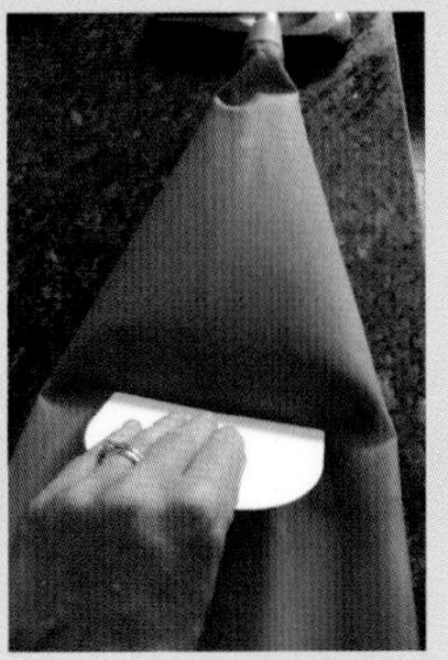

9 Pipe out the desired size of rounds (about 3cm [1"]) diameter for medium ones).

Press the nozzle right down on the paper then finish off with a flourish to obtain a nice round. Leave a good space between each round as they do spread out.

10 Leave for about 30 minutes to set (*croûter*). This helps to produce the feet (*pieds*) that make a macaron a macaron. You know they are ready to go into the oven when they feel cooked (hard) to the touch. Before they set you could decorate the shells with poppy/sesame seeds, cocoa powder, coconut etc.

Macarons can happily set for up to one hour. No need for any longer.

11 While they are setting you should preheat the oven to 160°C (325°F) fan (convection) oven setting.

If you do not have a fan oven you may need to make the temperature slightly higher.

Get to know your oven. All ovens are slightly different. If your macarons are not turning out as expected you could buy an oven thermometer to find out if your oven's settings are as accurate as they should be.

12 Bake in the centre of the oven – one tray at a time – for about 10–12 minutes.

Test after 8 minutes. Touch the top of a macaron and gently move your finger side to side. If there is a "wobble" cook for 3–4 minutes longer till firm.

When ready, leave on the baking tray until cool then scrape them all off carefully with a palette knife.

13 Marry up the discs in pairs on the baking parchment, one row flat side up and one row flat side down.

Prepare the piping bag with your chosen filling and pipe onto each upturned shell.

Then place its partner on top, using a circular motion to squash the shell down on the filling.

MACARON TIME!

- **Medium-sized** versions are perfect for *goûter* or tea time.
- **Mini macarons** can be served as *mignardises* (bite-sized desserts) at the end of a meal.
- **Mini-sized savoury** flavours are great for serving as unusual *apéritif* nibbles.
- **Giant** macarons are used as a base for pâtisserie desserts.
- **Mini** macarons will need about 8 minutes baking time.
- **Giant** macarons will need about 15 minutes, depending on your oven.
- For the **nut-free** version of this recipe see page 48.
- If the result isn't quite as perfect as you'd wanted, please read the basic recipe steps again, everything you need to know is here. Also consult **Troubleshooting**, page 129.

Macaron Fillings ...

... AND SOME SECRETS

The macaron's outer shells are sandwiched together with varied pastry cream mixes or a ganache (a mixture of chocolate and cream). For many macarons, you can simply sandwich them together with a dollop of jam. This is especially good for fruit macarons and ideal if you don't have much time. You can even use lemon curd instead of pastry cream for the lemon ones. It depends on your taste. Jam-filled macarons can be overly sweet, however. I think the fillings I have recommended in this book make the macarons very light and more of the kind you can find in good French pâtisseries. It takes more time, but you will discover it's worth it.

There are two secrets with the fillings. The first is not to fill the macarons too much – but don't be too sparing either. Ideally you need to see a hint of the filling completely covering the surface between the shells and there needs to be enough for the creamy mixture to penetrate into the meringue. That's the reason why you need to wait at least 24 hours before eating these delicacies.

The second secret is to make the filling as concentrated as you can, especially for pastry cream styles of fillings. I have reduced the sugar but added to the flavour as much as possible. Use superior quality extracts from good baking stores. Some specialised baking shops also sell natural flavourings – these are often available online. Also, adding a tiny amount of solid on top of the cream – such as a fine slice of glacé fruit or liquorice (or even chilli!) gives the macarons that extra *je ne sais quoi*.

You must leave macarons in the fridge for at least 24 hours before eating, as this lets the filling infuse into the shell. For chocolate ones, 36 hours is preferable. In addition, you must leave them at room temperature for 30 minutes before serving. This is what gives the macarons their typically scrumptious soft inside, while remaining crispy on the outside.

Bonne Dégustation !

AND DON'T FORGET...

If you do initially make some macarons that are not pretty enough to garnish, then you're still fashionable – you just can't lose. Even famous *chocolateries* tempt us on giant billboards with their latest sophisticated chocolates made with crushed macarons!

There are so many lovely desserts that would welcome them. Any dessert that asks for crushed amaretti biscuits for example, such as baked amaretti peaches (pictured below, recipe on MadAboutMacarons.com), would be ideal using crushed macarons in their place. Or simply use crushed macarons to garnish ice cream or chantilly with fresh fruit, put them in chocolate fondants, brownies or the humble crumble for that little extra something special.

PLAIN BUT FANCY

The following macarons are the straightforward classic flavours that everyone adores. You just *have* to start with these.

I have included suggestions for drinks to serve with all the macarons in this book. You can't go wrong with a pot of the "Champagne of teas" Darjeeling, a good cup of espresso coffee or treat yourself to a glass of off-dry Champagne with any of them.

Vanilla Macarons

MACARONS À LA VANILLE

150g organic egg whites
100g fine caster sugar
180g ground almonds
270g icing sugar
½ tsp vanilla powder (or seeds)
Yellow and caramel colouring

100g unsalted organic butter, softened
160ml (5 fl oz*) whole milk
1 vanilla pod, split lengthways
1 organic egg
20g caster sugar
20g custard powder (or cornflour and a few drops of vanilla extract, see page 128)
Few drops of vanilla extract (optional)

Vanilla goes well with Ceylon, Darjeeling or Keemun teas.

*US fluid ounces

There's nothing to beat this classic! You could call them "custard macarons", adding more yellow colouring and a dash of grated nutmeg. Add even more nutmeg and you have the taste of the delicious Portuguese custard tarts, *pasteis de nata*.

I recently made vanilla macarons for a party and the most satisfactory thrill was watching a 13-year-old taste her very first macaron. Taking the first dainty nibble, she was surprised that it was so soft inside. "I thought it was going to be like a custard cream biscuit but it's more like a marshmallow," she exclaimed. After a long satisfied "hmmm" she stuffed the rest in her mouth in one go.

* Follow the basic macaron recipe, adding a dash of yellow and caramel colouring. Add also ½ tsp of vanilla powder (or seeds) to the macaron mix.

* Cream the butter (the French refer to it as *en pommade*) and set aside. In a saucepan, boil the milk with the vanilla pod. Take off the heat, remove the pod and cut in half lengthways, scrape out the seeds and add to the milk. Leave the vanilla seeds and pod to infuse in the milk for about 20 minutes.

* In a bowl, beat together the egg, sugar and custard powder (or cornflour).

* Remove the vanilla pod from the milk and add the milk to the egg mix. Return to the pan and the heat, whisking constantly until it thickens, then take off the heat and cool. Place some clingfilm directly on the mixture so that no skin forms.

* When cool, whisk in the creamed butter, adding a few drops of vanilla extract to taste. Transfer to a piping bag, arrange the macaron shells in pairs, pipe filling onto one shell of each pair and assemble the macarons.

* Leave in the fridge for 24 hours before serving.

Coffee Macarons

MACARONS AU CAFÉ-CRÈME

150g organic egg whites
100g fine caster sugar
180g ground almonds
270g icing sugar
Caramel and yellow colouring

100g unsalted organic butter
160ml (5 fl oz*) whole milk
2 tbsps coffee granules
1 organic egg
20g caster sugar
20g custard powder (or cornflour and a few drops of vanilla extract, see page 128)
Few drops coffee extract

I like to taste this with tea, as coffee can be too overwhelming. Assam or Yunnan teas enhance the taste of coffee macarons.

Café-Crème is what the French drink in bowls in the mornings – our equivalent of a large mug of coffee with milk. What I learned at school as *café au lait*, has caused years of confusion (and amusement) in Parisian cafés. I should have been asking for a café-crème – yet normally there's no cream in it!

* Follow the basic macaron recipe, adding some caramel (or brown) with a dash of yellow colouring.
* To make the creamy filling, cream the butter and set aside. In a saucepan, boil the milk with the coffee.
* In a bowl, whisk together the egg, sugar and custard powder (or cornflour).
* Add the coffee and milk to the egg mix and return to the pan, stirring constantly until it thickens, then take off the heat and cool. Place some cling-film directly on the mixture so that no skin forms.
* When cool, mix in the softened, creamed butter and the coffee extract. Transfer to a piping bag, arrange the macaron shells in pairs, pipe filling onto one shell of each pair and assemble the macarons.
* Leave in the fridge for at least 24 hours before serving.

*US fluid ounces

Almond Macarons

MACARONS AUX AMANDES

150g organic egg whites
100g fine caster sugar
180g ground almonds
270g icing sugar
Flaked almonds (optional)

100g unsalted organic butter
160ml (5 fl oz*) whole milk
Few drops bitter almond extract
1 organic egg
20g caster sugar
20g custard powder (or cornflour and a few drops of vanilla extract, see page 128)

Serve with a good pot of tea such as Darjeeling or Assam. Alternatively serve with dessert wines such as Muscat or Sauternes or, if feeling luxuriously bubbly, a Champagne demi-sec.

This is a classic *parfum* (flavour) that does not require any colouring. However, as they are naturally white, you may wish to add a glittery dusting of gold lustre to them to add that *je ne sais quoi* for special occasions.

* Follow the basic macaron recipe. There's no need to add any colouring. You could also add some flaked almonds to the top of the macaron shells at *croûter* stage just before baking.
* To make the filling, cream the butter until it's light and fluffy and set aside.
* Boil the milk with the almond extract.
* In another bowl, whisk together the egg, sugar and custard powder.
* Pour the hot almond milk into the egg mixture and return to the pan, whisking constantly until it thickens, then take off the heat and cool. Place some clingfilm directly on the mixture so that no skin forms.
* When cool, beat in the softened creamed butter. Add more almond extract to taste, if necessary. Transfer to a piping bag, arrange the macaron shells in pairs, pipe filling onto one shell of each pair and assemble the macarons.
* Leave in the fridge for at least 24 hours before serving.

*US fluid ounces

Lemon Meringue Macarons

MACARONS AU CITRON MERINGUÉ

150g organic egg whites
100g fine caster sugar
180g ground almonds
270g icing sugar
Yellow colouring

100g unsalted organic butter, softened
160ml (5 fl oz*) whole milk
Few drops of lemon extract
1 organic egg
20g caster sugar
20g custard powder (or cornflour and a few drops of vanilla extract, see page 128)
Finely grated zest of an untreated lemon
40g glacé lemon or ginger (optional)

Delicious with Earl Grey, Lady Grey, Russian Earl Grey, or green teas. Alternatively, serve with light sparkling wines such as Vouvray, or Moscato d'Asti. If you're not into bubbles, then why not try a Riesling or Muscat dessert wine.

*US fluid ounces

Recently, a French friend gave his description on tasting these: *"It's like biting into a lemon meringue pie. You get the crispy meringue sensation, then the creamy lemon but it's lighter and healthier since you don't have the big pie crust."* On that note he helped himself to another ... and then another just to ensure his description was correct.

For extra-busy gourmets, you could assemble the macaron shells with a good quality lemon curd. Lemon and glacé (or crystallised) ginger also make a tangy combination.

* Follow the basic macaron recipe, adding a dash of yellow colouring.
* To make the creamy filling, cream the butter and set aside.
* Boil the milk with the lemon extract.
* In a bowl, whisk together the egg, sugar and custard powder (or cornflour).
* Incorporate the hot lemon milk to the egg mixture and return to the pan, whisking constantly until it thickens. Then take off the heat and cool. Place some cling-film directly on the mixture so that no skin forms.
* When cool, whisk in the softened, creamed butter and the finely grated lemon zest (ensure that it's the finest you can produce with a good microplane zester and be careful not to grate in the white pith underneath the skin, as this is bitter). Transfer to a piping bag. If using, garnish each macaron-half with finely chopped glacé lemon (or ginger) on top of the filling before putting the tops on.
* Leave in the fridge for at least 24 hours before serving.

Pistachio Macarons

MACARONS AUX PISTACHES

150g organic egg whites
100g fine caster sugar
180g ground almonds
270g icing sugar
Green and caramel (or yellow) colouring

100g unsalted organic butter, softened
160ml (5 fl oz*) whole milk
2 tbsps pistachio paste (or extra ground unsalted pistachios)
A few drops almond extract (optional)
30g ground unsalted pistachios
1 organic egg
20g sugar
20g custard powder (or cornflour and a few drops of vanilla extract, see page 128)

Serve this with an espresso coffee, to or Earl Grey, Darjeeling or green teas.

Don't forget to use unsalted pistachios for baking! Because pistachio paste can be difficult to obtain, you could replace this ingredient with more ground pistachios and a dash of bitter almond extract. Ground pistachios can be made by putting the unsalted whole nuts (without shells!) in a spice or coffee grinder.

* Follow the basic macaron recipe, adding a dash of green and caramel or yellow colouring (three parts green to one part caramel or yellow).

* Cream the butter and set aside.

* In a saucepan, bring the milk, pistachio paste and ground pistachios to near boiling. (If you have no pistachio paste, add extra ground pistachios and a few drops of almond extract.)

* In a bowl, whisk together the egg, sugar and custard powder (or cornflour).

* Add the pistachio milk to the egg mix and return to the pan, whisking constantly until it thickens, then take off the heat and cool. Place some cling-film directly on the mixture so that no skin forms.

* When cool, mix in the creamed butter and transfer to a piping bag. Arrange the macaron shells in pairs, pipe filling onto one shell of each pair and assemble the macarons.

* Leave in the fridge for at least 24 hours before serving.

*US fluid ounces

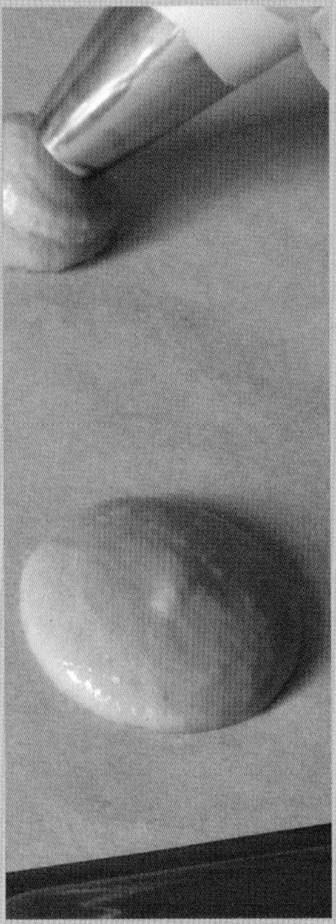
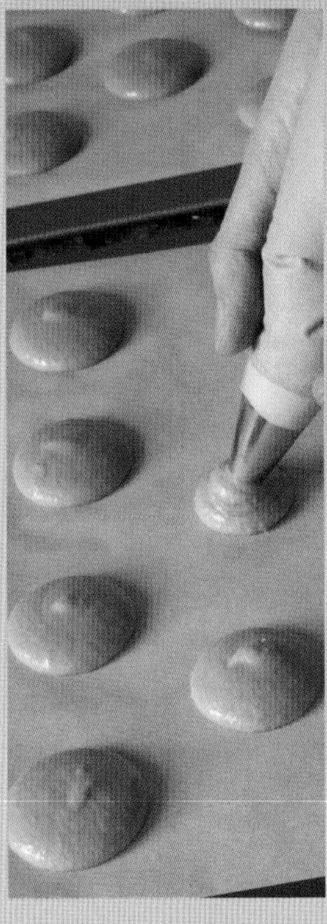

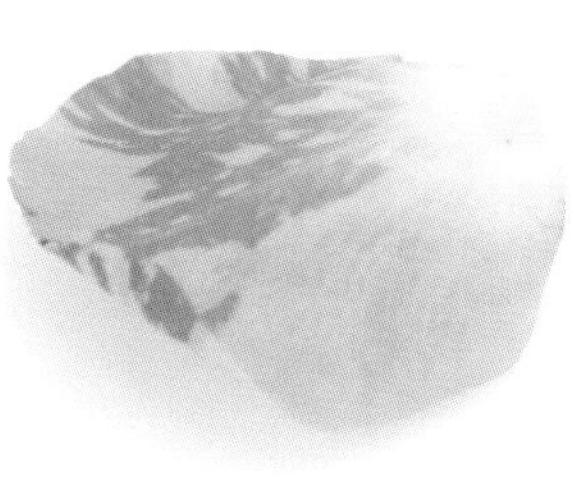

Rose Macarons

MACARONS À LA ROSE

150g organic egg whites
100g fine caster sugar
180g ground almonds
270g icing sugar
Red colouring

100g unsalted organic butter, softened
90ml (3 fl oz*) single cream
5 tbsps rosewater (water with essense of rose no more than about 6%)
1 organic egg
20g caster sugar
10g cornflour
Few drops of rose extract (optional)

For a truly luxurious, toe-curling treat these are divine served with pink Champagne.

Rose macarons can make a stunning visual impact but their flavour is equally impressive. Lychees also go well with rose so you could add half a lychee on top of the cream before assembling the top half. For special occasions why not add sugar roses for decoration. Some brands labelled "rosewater" are in fact pure essence, or essence and alcohol. Five tablespoons of that would be unbearably pungent! My rose macarons use rosewater made from water with added essence no more than about 6%. If you've bought essence, you only need a few drops.

* Follow the basic macaron recipe, adding a dash of red colouring. (You could pipe out the macarons into love-heart shapes. Simply pipe them out with two strokes of the piping bag nozzle. Adjust the cooking time if they are the 6–7cm (2") diameter of giant macarons and cook for nearer 15 minutes.)
* For the filling, cream the butter and set aside.
* Heat the cream and rosewater in a saucepan.
* In a bowl, whisk the egg and the sugar until white and creamy. Whisk in the cornflour. Pour the hot rose-cream into the cornflour mixture and mix well.
* Return to the pan, whisking briskly until the cream thickens, then take off the heat and cool. Place some clingfilm directly on the mixture so that no skin forms.
* When the rose mixture is cool, add the rose extract, if using, then whisk in the creamed butter and transfer to a piping bag. Arrange the macaron shells in pairs, pipe filling onto one shell of each pair and assemble the macarons.
* Leave in the fridge for at least 24 hours before serving.

*US fluid ounces

Dark Chocolate Macarons

MACARONS AU CHOCOLAT NOIR

150g organic egg whites
100g fine caster sugar
180g ground almonds
270g icing sugar
10g unsweetened cocoa powder
Brown colouring (optional)

200g dark cooking chocolate (at least 64% cocoa solids)
1 tsp coffee granules
190g whipping cream
50g unsalted organic butter, softened and cut into cubes
Cocoa powder or icing or melted chocolate to decorate (optional)

Serve these with an espresso or macchiato coffee, or Earl Grey or rooibos tea. If serving at the end of a meal, serve with a dessert wine such as Rivesaltes, Banyuls, Maury or Rasteau. For red wine lovers, pick a mellow red with not too much tannin, such as a Merlot. Alternatively, enjoy with an orange liqueur such as Grand Marnier or a single-malt whisky.

Chocolate is usually everyone's favourite. Adding a dash of coffee to dark chocolate brings out its intense aroma.

I know it looks precise to use 10g of cocoa powder, but, believe me, if you add more the macaron shell does become tricky to work with, and the centres don't cook so well. This is why you need digital scales! You could also replace the cocoa powder with some brown colouring.

* Follow the basic macaron recipe, adding 10g unsweetened cocoa powder to the mix. You could also add a touch of brown colouring with a hint of red to give that intense chocolate look.

* To make the ganache, break the chocolate into a bowl. Heat the cream and coffee until nearly boiling then pour over the broken chocolate.

* Stir constantly in the middle with a wooden spoon or hand whisk until smooth. Add the butter to make a beautifully glossy ganache.

* Leave to cool, but be careful not to wait too long as the chocolate hardens quite quickly. Transfer to a piping bag, arrange the macaron shells in pairs, pipe filling onto one shell of each pair and assemble the macarons.

* For that final touch, dust the tops of the macarons with cocoa powder or dip half of each macaron in melted chocolate.

* Leave in the fridge for at least 24 hours, preferably 36 hours. Take out of the fridge one hour before serving.

Nut-free Moka Macarons

MACARONS MOKA (POUR ALLERGIQUES AUX FRUITS À COQUE)

150g organic egg whites
90g fine caster sugar
100g quinoa flakes (organic, pre-cooked)
240g icing sugar
10g unsweetened cocoa powder (optional)

200g dark cooking chocolate (at least 64% cocoa solids)
3 tsps coffee granules
190g whipping cream
50g unsalted organic butter, softened and cut into cubes

Serve these with a good espresso coffee or a macchiato. For tea-lovers, serve with Darjeeling, Earl Grey or Rooibos.

At my daughter's last birthday party, a frustrated wee soul exclaimed: "I'm not allowed to eat any of the macarons on the table because they contain nuts." It was maddening for her to watch everyone around her tuck in to the pile of macarons. So it became the ultimate challenge, to create a nut-free macaron! I have used quinoa (pronounced *keen-wah*), a grain-like seed that is not only nut-free, but also gluten-free with countless healthy benefits. Quinoa has a nutty/seedy taste so a chocolate-moka ganache is the perfect complement.

* Follow the basic macaron recipe, using the quantities above and replace the ground almonds with quinoa flakes. Grind the quinoa flakes to a powder either in a coffee grinder, blender or with a mortar and pestle. You could add 10g unsweetened cocoa powder to the mix for chocolate shells. Ensure that you leave the quinoa macarons to rest for 1 hour 30 minutes before baking. Follow the method of the basic recipe as you would for normal macarons and for timings and temperatures.

* To make the ganache, break the chocolate into a bowl. Heat the cream and coffee until nearly boiling then pour over the broken chocolate.

* Stir constantly in the middle with a wooden spoon or hand whisk until smooth. Add the butter to make a beautifully glossy ganache.

* Leave to cool, but be careful not to wait too long as the chocolate hardens quite quickly. Transfer to a piping bag, arrange the macaron shells in pairs, pipe filling onto one shell of each pair and assemble the macarons.

* Leave in the fridge for at least 24 hours, preferably 36, before serving.

* Do ensure that everyone knows these macarons are nut-free. Decorate them differently from other macarons. For example, you could write "nut-free" using a liquid food colouring pâtisserie pen (see Stockists page 127).

CHOCOLATE COMBINATIONS

The beauty with chocolate is that you can concoct your own matching flavour combinations. There is practically no end to the possible additions you can try, just like the top French pâtisserie chefs. Alternatively, keeping it classic and simple is equally delicious.

For example, chocolate-orange works well. Simply use the classic chocolate macaron recipe, add the zest of an untreated orange to the ganache and some orange extract, or a dash of Grand Marnier for something "adult".

Take another classic like chocolate-mint and add peppermint extract and a few chopped fresh mint leaves.

For the more adventurous, if you like chocolate-chilli combinations, add a good pinch of cayenne pepper to the ganache filling. Or try a good pinch of ground szechuan pepper for a touch of the exotic.

Chocolate-Beetroot Macarons

MACARONS CHOCOLAT-BETTERAVE

150g organic egg whites
100g fine caster sugar
180g ground almonds
270g icing sugar
Red and blue colouring

200g dark cooking chocolate (at least 64% cocoa solids)
180g whipping cream (at least 30% fat)
2 drops of ginger extract
40g unsalted organic butter, softened and cut into cubes
100g cooked beetroot, finely grated

Serve with milky coffees or teas such as Earl Grey, Assam, Darjeeling or Yunnan. If you serve them at the end of a meal then go for something original like ginger wine (the ginger brings out the chocolate and beetroot!) or a Whisky Mac.

The children adore this and it was the first flavour to disappear at the latest birthday party. I make a gooey chocolate and beetroot fondant cake that is a surprising hit – and so transformed it into a macaron. You don't really taste the beetroot that much. It just adds a depth to the colour in the chocolate, and the sensation of biting into the beetroot is intriguing. It's also an imaginative way to get your kids to eat their vegetables!

If you do buy already-cooked beetroot, get it as fresh as possible and, of course, without the vinegar.

* Make macaron shells using red colouring with a dash of blue (or bright raspberry or fuchsia colouring) for a lovely shiny beetroot colour.
* To make the ganache, break the chocolate into small pieces into a bowl. In a saucepan, bring the cream to nearly boiling point with the ginger extract, then pour over the broken chocolate.
* Stir constantly in the middle with a wooden spoon or whisk until smooth. Add butter to make the ganache beautifully glossy. Add the finely grated cooked beetroot and mix thoroughly.
* Leave to cool but be careful not to wait too long as the chocolate hardens quite quickly. Transfer to a piping bag, arrange the macaron shells in pairs, pipe filling onto one shell of each pair and assemble the macarons.
* Leave in the fridge for at least 24 hours, preferably 36, before serving.

Chocolate-Caramel Macarons

MACARONS CHOCOLAT-CARAMEL

150g organic egg whites
100g fine caster sugar
180g ground almonds
270g icing sugar
Caramel colouring

170g pâtisserie milk chocolate and caramel bar
140g whipping cream
30g unsalted organic butter, softened and cut into cubes
Pinch of sea salt

Serve with Assam, Darjeeling, Earl Grey or Ceylon teas. Also good with a cappuccino or latte coffee. If serving at the end of a meal, they go well with dessert wines such as Rivesaltes Ambré, an Alsace Riesling (late harvest) or a tawny port.

This recipe is wicked and made easier with ready-made caramel cooking chocolate.

If you can't find chocolate-caramel cooking chocolate, then use milk cooking chocolate, only 100g whipping cream and 40g of caramel syrup instead. Alternatively replace half of the chocolate with Willie's Supreme Cacao 100% "Javan Light Breaking" which has a caramel note.

* Follow the basic macaron recipe, adding some caramel colouring. Alternatively, you could follow the same recipe making chocolate shells, in which case add 10g unsweetened cocoa powder.

* To make the ganache, break the chocolate into small pieces into a bowl. In a saucepan, heat the cream then pour over the broken chocolate.

* Stir constantly in the middle with a wooden spoon until smooth (about 5 minutes). Add the butter to make the ganache beautifully glossy, then add the salt.

* Leave to cool in the fridge for at least an hour.

* Transfer to a piping bag, arrange the macaron shells in pairs, pipe filling onto one shell of each pair and assemble the macarons.

* For extra effect, melt some extra chocolate (about three little cubes) and, using a teaspoon, quickly dribble the chocolate over the finished macarons to decorate as in the photo.

* Leave in the fridge for at least 24 hours before serving.

Chocolate, Cardamom and Ginger Macarons

MACARONS AU CHOCOLAT, CARDAMOME ET GINGEMBRE

150g organic egg whites
100g fine caster sugar
180g ground almonds
270g icing sugar
10g unsweetened cocoa powder
4g powdered ginger

200g dark chocolate (at least 64% cocoa solids)
190g whipping cream
Few drops of ginger extract
10 cardamom pods, crushed
50g unsalted organic butter, softened and cut into cubes
1 tbsp glacé ginger, finely chopped

Serve this health-boosting macaron with a good espresso coffee. For tea-drinkers, serve with Assam, Darjeeling or Earl Grey. For real spice lovers, then serve with a Chai. If serving at the end of a meal, then enjoy with a tawny port, single-malt whisky or a brandy mixed with a dash of Green Ginger wine.

I love the mixture of bitter chocolate and ginger but the addition of exotic cardamom just adds that extra surprising kick. Cardamom is believed to be a slimming agent so, combined with a boost of magnesium from the chocolate, you are giving yourself the boost you deserve for that luxurious and healthy afternoon tea. Ginger helps digestion, keeps colds at bay, has anti-inflammatory properties and is even said to boost virility!

For **Chocolate-Ginger Macarons**: omit cardamom and add an extra tablespoon of glacé ginger to the ganache. For duo-colour macarons, half chocolate, half ginger: use half the quantity for each (see page 126). For the ginger halves, 2 parts caramel to 1 part yellow colouring, and 2g powdered ginger.

* Follow the basic macaron recipe, but add 10g cocoa powder (or brown colouring) and 4g of powdered ginger to the mix.

* To make the ganache, break the chocolate into small pieces into a bowl. In a saucepan, heat the cream with the ginger extract and cardamom pods for several minutes. Sieve out the pods then pour the cream over the chocolate.

* Stir constantly in the middle with a wooden spoon until smooth. Add the butter to make the ganache beautifully glossy. Add the finely chopped glacé (crystallised) ginger. Try to use a good quality one that isn't sugar coated.

* Leave to cool, but be careful not to wait too long as the chocolate hardens quite quickly. Transfer to a piping bag, arrange the macaron shells in pairs, pipe filling onto one shell of each pair. Add a square bit of glacé ginger to the middle of each macaron before putting on their tops.

* Leave in the fridge for at least 24 hours, preferably 36, before serving.

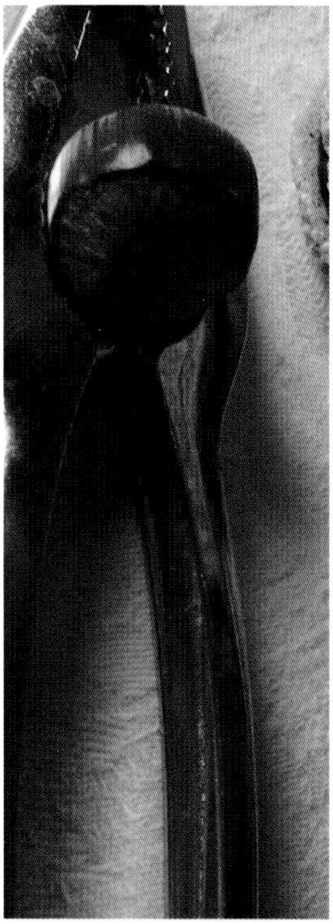

Hazelnut and Chocolate Macarons

MACARONS NOISETTES ET CHOCOLAT

150g organic egg whites
100g fine caster sugar
120g ground almonds
60g finely ground hazelnuts
270g icing sugar

200g dark cooking chocolate (at least 64% cocoa solids)
190g whipping cream
1 tsp coffee granules
20g ground hazelnuts
40g unsalted organic butter, softened and cut into cubes

Serve with Darjeeling tea or a good espresso coffee.

If you prefer macarons with no colouring, then this is one of the ideal flavours for you. Chocolate, hazelnut and almond macarons are naturally coloured.

* Follow the basic macaron recipe, adding the 60g of finely ground hazelnuts.

* To make the ganache, break the chocolate into small pieces into a bowl. In a saucepan, bring the cream and coffee to near boiling point then pour over the broken chocolate.

* Stir constantly in the middle with a wooden spoon until smooth. Add the butter to make the ganache beautifully glossy then stir in the 20g of ground hazelnuts. (You could use a praline dark chocolate bar instead).

* Leave to cool, but be careful not to wait too long as the chocolate hardens quite quickly. Transfer to a piping bag, arrange the macaron shells in pairs, pipe filling onto one shell of each pair and assemble the macarons.

* Leave in the fridge for at least 24 hours, preferably 36, before serving.

TIPS

Alternatively, pipe out tiny versions of the macarons.
They are ideal served as *mignardises* at the end of a meal.

Or serve them without the chocolate ganache as an apéritif (use the reduced-sugar, savoury basic ingredients for the shells – see reference chart, page 126) with foie gras and a soupçon of fig jam.

The giant versions are excellent for dessert with, for example, tiramisu cream.

Chocolate and Lapsang Souchong Macarons

MACARONS AU CHOCOLAT ET THÉ FUMÉ

150g organic egg whites
100g fine caster sugar
180g ground almonds
270g icing sugar
10g unsweetened cocoa powder

200g dark cooking chocolate (at least 64% cocoa)
190g whipping cream
2 Lapsang Souchong tea bags
2 tbsps whisky
40g unsalted organic butter, softened and cut into cubes

Serve with Lapsang Souchong tea (or whatever tea you infuse in the ganache). Alternatively, enjoy with a peaty single-malt whisky.

Highly perfumed teas are delicious added to chocolate – just infuse the tea when heating the cream for the ganache. Here I've used Lapsang Souchong (smoked tea) but Earl Grey tea is also a lovely combination (just omit the whisky). I also like to infuse South African Rooibos tea in the cream (caffeine-free, antioxidant red tea with a nutty taste).

* Follow the basic macaron recipe, adding 10g unsweetened cocoa powder to the mix.

* To make the ganache, break the chocolate into small pieces into a bowl. In a saucepan, heat the cream with the tea, then take off the heat to infuse for 10 minutes. Add the whisky and bring the cream nearly to the boil, remove the tea bags then pour over the broken chocolate.

* Stir constantly in the middle with a wooden spoon until smooth. Add the butter to make the ganache beautifully glossy.

* Leave to cool but be careful not to wait too long as the chocolate hardens quite quickly. Transfer to a piping bag, arrange the macaron shells in pairs, pipe filling onto one shell of each pair and assemble the macarons.

* Leave in the fridge for at least 24 hours, preferably 36, before serving.

Pistachio and Dark Chocolate Macarons

MACARONS PISTACHE-CHOCOLAT NOIR

150g organic egg whites
100g fine caster sugar
180g ground almonds
270g icing sugar
Green and caramel colouring

200g dark cooking chocolate (at least 64% cocoa)
190g whipping cream
30g freshly ground unsalted pistachios (whizzed up in a spice/coffee grinder)
1 tbsp pistachio paste (or extra ground pistachios and a few drops almond extract)
50g unsalted organic butter, softened and cut into cubes

Serve with an espresso coffee or latte.

These are possibly the quickest and easiest macarons to make and are a firm favourite with family and friends. You could make duo-colour macaron shells and decorate them with melted chocolate using your artistic flair.

* Follow the basic macaron recipe, adding a dash of green and caramel colouring (three parts green to one part caramel).

* To make the ganache, break the chocolate into small pieces into a bowl. In a saucepan, bring the cream to near boiling point with the pistachio paste and the ground pistachios. (If you have no pistachio paste add extra ground pistachios and a few drops of almond extract.) Then pour over the broken chocolate.

* Stir constantly in the middle with a wooden spoon until smooth. Add butter to make the ganache beautifully glossy.

* Leave to cool but be careful not to wait too long as the chocolate hardens quite quickly. Transfer to a piping bag, arrange the macaron shells in pairs, pipe filling onto one shell of each pair and assemble the macarons.

* Leave in the fridge for at least 24 hours, preferably 36, before serving.

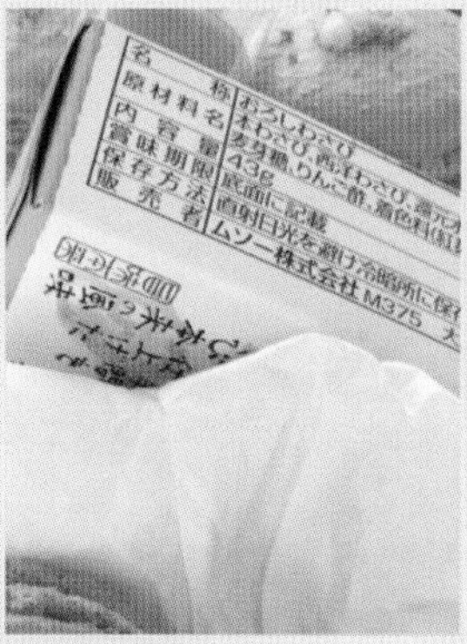
名称 おろしわさび
原材料名 本わさび、西洋わさび
内容量 43g
賞味期限 底面に記載
保存方法 直射日光を避け冷暗所に
販売者 ムソー株式会社 M375

Pistachio, White Chocolate and Wasabi Macarons

MACARONS AU PISTACHE, CHOCOLAT BLANC ET WASABI

150g organic egg whites
100g fine caster sugar
180g ground almonds
270g icing sugar
Green and caramel colouring

130g coconut milk*
30g ground pistachios
10g wasabi*
170g white chocolate*

Ideally, serve this with green tea, otherwise vanilla tea will match the flavours well.

Inspired by an ice cream dessert I tasted recently, this beautifully translates into a wild and wicked wasabi macaron.

* Follow the basic macaron recipe, adding a dash of green and caramel colouring (three parts green to one part caramel).

* To make the ganache, in a saucepan, heat the coconut milk and ground pistachios. Take a little of the liquid and blend with the wasabi. Add the wasabi to the coconut milk.

* Break the white chocolate into bits and add to the coconut milk mix, over a medium heat, stirring constantly with a wooden spoon until glossy and smooth.

* Leave to cool in the fridge for at least an hour until the chocolate is manageable. Transfer to a piping bag, arrange the macaron shells in pairs, pipe filling onto one shell of each pair and assemble the macarons.

* Leave in the fridge for at least 24 hours before serving.

* If following a gluten-free diet check ingredients of these products

CREATE A STORM WITH YOUR TEACUP

Now that you've mastered the chocolate macarons, you can impress family and friends further with even more variations.

The beauty of the macaron is that you can adapt just about any flavour you like to it. So enjoy trying out your own tastes based on these recipe ideas. (In fact, I'm still experimenting with more mad macaron varieties!)

Relish them with your afternoon tea break, known as *goûter*, here in France. It's an institution – often referred to as "quatre heures" as it is served around 4 o'clock when the children come home from school. As my French husband says, there should be nothing apart from the goûter between meals (no snacking!). The macaron is a perfect goûter time treat. It provides that decadently sweet but light boost with a touch of sophistication to tide you over until dinner. When I need a macaron fix and there are none to hand, I just sneak one or two different *parfums* out of my precious macaron "bank" in the freezer.

Experiment and indulge!

Marmalade Macarons

MACARONS AU CITRON ET CONFIT D'ORANGE

150g organic egg whites
100g fine caster sugar
180g ground almonds
270g icing sugar
Orange colouring
Few drops lemon extract

100g unsalted organic butter, softened
160ml (5 fl oz*) whole milk
Few drops of lemon extract
1 organic egg
20g sugar
20g custard powder (or cornflour and a few drops of vanilla extract, see page 128)
Zest of an untreated lemon, finely grated
40g candied orange peel

Lovely with Earl Grey or Darjeeling tea. Or serve with a Gewürztraminer wine (even better, a "late harvest" vintage) at the end of a meal.

*US fluid ounces

These are handy if you've made a batch of lemon macarons and want to make another flavour but don't have that much time: just make a small batch of orange shells, use the lemon cream and add some glacé orange peel for an alternative. For a more orange macaron, then replace the lemon zest and extract with orange zest and extract.

* Follow the basic macaron recipe, adding a dash of orange colouring and some lemon extract. You could also make a duo-colour macaron, using one lemon shell and one orange shell.

* To make the cream filling, cream the butter and set aside.

* In a saucepan, boil the milk with the lemon extract. In a bowl, whisk together the egg, sugar and custard powder.

* Incorporate the hot cream into the egg mix and return to the pan and the heat, stirring constantly until it thickens. Then take off the heat and cool. Place some cling film directly on the mixture so that no skin forms.

* When cool, mix in the creamed butter and the lemon zest.

* Transfer to a piping bag. Arrange the macaron shells in pairs, pipe filling onto one shell of each pair. To garnish, place finely chopped candied orange peel on top of the piped cream before assembling.

* Leave in the fridge for at least 24 hours before serving.

Cranachan Macarons

MACARONS FRAMBOISE, WHISKY ET MIEL DE BRUYERE

150g organic egg whites
100g fine caster sugar
180g ground almonds
270g icing sugar
Red colouring

100g butter, softened
30g heather honey
1 organic egg
10g cornflour
50g whisky
50g whipping cream
100g fresh raspberries, crushed to a purée
10g fine oatmeal (optional, contains gluten)

Needless to say, serve with a dram, a Whisky Mac or an Irish Coffee.

You'll be hard pushed to find this Scottish-inspired flavour in a Parisian pâtisserie! The ingredients here are of course influenced by the traditional Scottish dessert made with fresh raspberries, fresh cream, oatmeal, whisky and honey. Our filling here is a pastry cream rather than a fresh cream.

* Follow the basic macaron recipe, adding a good dash of red colouring for a bright raspberry colour. You could also make a duo macaron – half deep pink and the other uncoloured. Sprinkle with a few flakes of oats.
* To make the cream filling, cream the butter and set aside.
* Whisk together the honey with the egg until creamy, then add the cornflour and continue whisking to mix well.
* In a saucepan, heat the whisky, cream and raspberry purée together. Pour this over the egg mix and quickly then transfer back to the pan and the heat. Whisk constantly on a lower heat until thickened. Set aside to cool and mix in the oatmeal if you are using it (it contains gluten).
* Gradually whisk in the creamed butter.
* Transfer to a piping bag, arrange the macaron shells in pairs, pipe filling onto one shell of each pair and assemble.
* Leave in the fridge for at least 24 hours before serving.

Vanilla, Lemon, Poppy Seed & Cinnamon Macarons

MACARONS VANILLE, CITRON, PAVOT ET CANNELLE

150g organic egg whites
100g fine caster sugar
180g ground almonds
270g icing sugar
Yellow colouring
1 tsp vanilla powder (or seeds)
Poppy seeds (for decoration)

100g unsalted organic butter
160ml (5 fl oz*) whole milk
1 vanilla pod, cut lengthways
1 organic egg
20g sugar
1 tbsp rum
2 tsps ground cinnamon
20g custard powder (or cornflour and a few drops of vanilla extract, see page 128)
Zest of an untreated lemon
1 tbsp poppy seeds

Delicious with Earl Grey or Darjeeling tea.

*US fluid ounces

Inspired by Kalàcs, the decadent pastries from Eastern Europe, here's a macaron version which includes a dash of cinnamon and rum which add a subtle and unique flavour.

* Follow the basic macaron recipe, adding a dash of yellow colouring plus the vanilla powder (or seeds). At *croûter* stage, you could decorate with some poppy seeds.

* For the cream filling, cream the butter and set aside.

* In a saucepan, boil the milk with the vanilla pod, cut in half lengthways. Take off the heat and leave to infuse for 20 minutes. Scrape out the seeds and then discard the vanilla pod.

* In a bowl, whisk together the egg, sugar, rum, 1 tsp of the cinnamon powder and the custard powder.

* Pour this mixture into the egg mix and then return to the saucepan on the heat, stirring constantly until it thickens. Take off the heat and cool. Place some cling-film directly on the mixture so that no skin forms.

* When cool, mix in softened, creamed butter, the poppy seeds and the lemon zest. Transfer to a piping bag, arrange the macaron shells in pairs, pipe filling onto one shell of each pair and assemble.

* To decorate, sprinkle with an extra dusting of cinnamon.

* Leave in the fridge for at least 24 hours before serving.

Liquorice and White Chocolate Macarons

MACARONS À LA REGLISSE ET CHOCOLAT BLANC

150g organic egg whites
100g fine caster sugar
180g ground almonds
270g icing sugar
Concentrated black food colouring paste

100g whipping cream
170g white chocolate*
30g Antesite aniseed concentrate (or as much liquorice flavouring or aniseed-flavoured alcohol, e.g. Pernod, Ricard, as you prefer)
30g plain liquorice candy stick*

Good with Yunnan or Darjeeling teas.

The sensation of a bite into this liquorice macaron reminds me of when I was little, dipping into a liquorice sherbet. I used to get one of these when I was at my granny's if I was particularly good.

Here the mix of liquorice and white chocolate doesn't give you the fizz in the mouth, but the explosion of the two flavours amounts to the same luxury.

* Follow the basic macaron recipe, adding a good dash of black food colouring paste to the whites at the end of whisking. For duo-colour macarons, make two half-quantities of the mixture and only colour one at meringue stage.

* To make the ganache filling, heat the cream in a saucepan. Break the white chocolate into pieces and add to the cream. Once melted, add in the aniseed concentrate (or liquorice flavouring) stirring constantly until you have a nice smooth consistency.

* Take off the heat and cool in the fridge for at least an hour (white chocolate can be runny and syrupy and otherwise difficult to handle so keep checking its consistency to make it manageable).

* When the chocolate is cooled, transfer to a piping bag. Arrange the macaron shells in pairs (one black, one white), pipe filling onto one shell of each pair.

* Cut the liquorice stick into fine slices. Garnish with a slice of liquorice on top of the filling and then assemble.

* Leave in the fridge for at least 24 hours before serving.

* If following a gluten-free diet check ingredients of these products

A.MONTEUX
VALLAURIS

Orange Blossom Macarons

MACARONS À LA FLEUR D'ORANGER

These delicately perfumed macarons would, as a dessert, nicely complement a Moroccan-style meal of tagine or couscous.

150g organic egg whites
100g fine caster sugar
180g ground almonds
270g icing sugar
Yellow and red colouring

100g unsalted organic butter, softened
90ml (3 fl oz) single cream
5 tbsps orange flower water
1 organic egg
20g caster sugar
10g cornflour
2–3 drops of orange blossom extract (optional)
Icing sugar to decorate

* Follow the basic macaron recipe, adding a dash of yellow and red colouring.

* To make the cream filling, cream the butter and set aside.

* In a saucepan, heat the cream and orange flower water till almost boiling.

* In a bowl, whisk the egg and the sugar until white and creamy and mix in the cornflour. Pour the orange flower cream onto the egg mixture.

* Transfer back to the pan and the heat, whisking briskly until the cream thickens, then take off the heat and cool.

* When the mixture is cool, add the extract and beat in the softened, creamed butter. Transfer to a piping bag, arrange the macaron shells in pairs, pipe filling onto one shell of each pair and assemble.

* Leave in the fridge for at least 24 hours before serving. To decorate, sprinkle with a dusting of icing sugar.

Beautiful served with a glass of Sauternes dessert wine after a meal. Otherwise, they're a real treat in the afternoon with a cup of Earl Grey, Lady Grey, Russian Earl Grey, oolong or orange blossom tea.

Prune, Armagnac and Orange Macarons

MACARONS PRUNEAUX, ARMAGNAC, ORANGES

150g organic egg whites
100g fine caster sugar
180g ground almonds
270g icing sugar
Orange (red/yellow) colouring
Black colouring

200ml orange juice
250g prunes
3 tbsps Armagnac
Few drops of vanilla extract
Zest and juice of an untreated orange
Candied orange peel (optional)

Serve for afternoon tea with a pot of Russian Earl Grey or Lady Grey. Or serve at the end of a meal with a chilled Muscat wine or with an orange liqueur such as Grand Marnier or Cointreau served on crushed ice.

These macarons were inspired by a Corsican speciality: sugar-coated soft dried prunes stuffed with candied orange peel. The filling is healthy since there is no added sugar, except for the natural fruit sugars. For busy gourmets you could simply use a ready-made prune paste and add some orange zest.

* Follow the basic macaron recipe, adding a dash of red and yellow colouring to make a vivid orange colour. At *croûter* stage, using a paintbrush, splash with some black food colouring for a dramatic effect.

* For the filling, heat the orange juice and prunes in a covered pan until the prunes are tender. Drain off and reserve the juice. Pit the prunes once they are cool enough to do so.

* To a saucepan, add the Armagnac, vanilla extract, reserved juice, pitted prunes and zest, then cook gently for 20 minutes.

* Cool. Purée the mixture and transfer to a piping bag. Arrange the macaron shells in pairs, pipe filling onto one shell of each pair. You could also add some chopped candied orange peel before assembling.

* Leave in the fridge for at least 24 hours before serving.

Tiramisu Macarons

MACARONS TIRAMISU

150g organic egg whites
100g fine caster sugar
180g ground almonds
270g icing sugar
Yellow and caramel colouring (optional)

130g whipping cream
2 tbsps coffee powder
170g white chocolate
Few drops bitter almond extract
Cocoa powder to decorate (optional)

If serving at the end of a meal, try them with a coffee liqueur or perhaps an Amaretto. Otherwise they go beautifully with most cuppas: Darjeeling, Assam teas, or cappuccino, latte or espresso coffees.

Tiramisu is always a popular dessert. Why not try my macaron version of this classic, made with a coffee, white chocolate and almond ganache. You can add caramel colouring but the shells look equally nice uncoloured and dusted in cocoa powder before serving.

* Follow the basic macaron recipe, adding a dash of caramel and yellow colouring if you wish.
* To make the ganache, heat the cream with the coffee in a saucepan. Break up the chocolate and melt in a bowl over a pan of boiling water (*bain-marie*) and gradually add the cream. Add the almond extract. (For a quick alternative: melt the chocolate, coffee powder and cream in the microwave, three times for 30 seconds each time, mixing well after each.)
* Leave to cool in the fridge for about an hour. Keep checking that it has the right consistency, as white chocolate is runnier than dark chocolate and so much easier to work with if chilled (but not hard).
* Transfer to a piping bag, arrange the macaron shells in pairs, pipe filling onto one shell of each pair and assemble.
* Leave in the fridge for at least 24 hours before serving. Decorate with a dusting of cocoa powder just before serving.

Tutti-Frutti Macarons

MACARONS AUX FRUITS ROUGES

150g organic egg whites
100g fine caster sugar
180g ground almonds
270g icing sugar
Blue and red colouring
Black colouring or poppy seeds

100g organic butter, softened
10g cornflour
1 egg, beaten
100ml (3.5 fl oz*) liquidised mix of raspberry, strawberry and blueberry (or a red fruit smoothie, not frozen, already prepared)
2 tbsps crème de cassis (blackcurrant syrup)

Serve with Earl Grey, Ceylon or Yunnan teas.

You could decorate the meringue shells with poppy seeds before they go in the oven or with a splash of black food colouring as pictured.

In place of the blackcurrant syrup you could use raspberry, strawberry or even violet syrup. Over to you!

* Follow the basic macaron recipe, adding a dash of red and blue colouring. At *croûter* stage, using a paintbrush, splash with some black food colouring for a dramatic effect.

* For the filling, cream the butter and set aside.

* Whisk the cornflour and beaten egg. Heat the smoothie and crème de cassis together then add to the cornflour mix, then move back to the heat, whisking continuously until creamy and thickened.

* Once cool, whisk in the creamed butter. Transfer to a piping bag, arrange the macaron shells in pairs, pipe filling onto one shell of each pair and assemble.

* Leave in the fridge for at least 24 hours before serving.

*US fluid ounces

Whisky MacCoffee

MACARONS WHISKY-CAFÉ

150g organic egg whites
100g fine caster sugar
180g ground almonds
270g icing sugar
Caramel colouring

100g unsalted butter, softened
20g caster sugar
1 organic egg
10g cornflour
80ml (2.5 fl oz*) whisky
40ml (1 fl oz*) espresso coffee
Melted chocolate to decorate

Rather than Darjeeling, serve with a dram or a Whisky Mac or just on its own with some mineral water like the Scots.

Needless to say as a Scot, I had to see if a "Whisky Mac" would work as a macaron and it's delicious.

* Follow the basic macaron recipe, adding a dash of caramel or brown colouring.

* For the filling, cream the butter and set aside. Whisk together the sugar with the egg until creamy, then add the cornflour and mix well.

* Heat the whisky and coffee together in a pan. Take off the heat and pour over the egg mix, then transfer back to the pan. Whisk constantly on a lower heat until thickened. Set aside to cool.

* Blend with the creamed butter. Transfer to a piping bag, arrange the macaron shells in pairs, pipe filling onto one shell of each pair and assemble. You could decorate the final macarons with melted chocolate dribbled finely (and quickly) to create a tartan effect.

* Leave in the fridge for at least 24 hours before serving.

*US fluid ounces

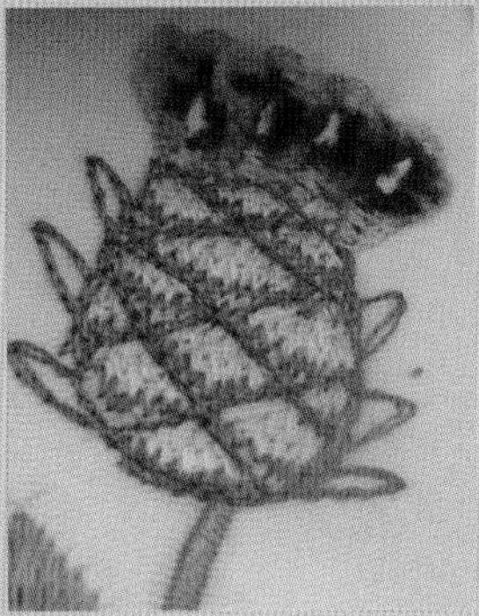

Sticky Toffee Macarons

MACARONS "STICKY TOFFEE PUDDING"

150g organic egg whites
100g fine caster sugar
180g ground almonds
270g icing sugar
Brown colouring

400g soft dates, pitted and chopped
60g unsalted organic butter
2 tbsps dark rum
½ tsp mixed spice powder
2 tbsps golden syrup (substitute
2 tbsps brown sugar if you can't
get golden syrup, see page 128)
Few drops of vanilla extract
120ml (4 fl oz*) double cream

Serve with Assam, Ceylon, Darjeeling or Oolong teas.
If serving with wine, they go well with a late harvest Riesling or other dessert wines such as a Rivesaltes Ambré or Monbazillac.

Anytime my children go to Britain to visit Granny and Grandpa, they have a good dose (if not overdose) of Sticky Toffee Pudding, as we poor STP fans cannot buy this in France. It goes without saying that I felt the urge to convert the classic pud into a macaron. The good news is that it is still as sticky but is gluten free!

* Follow the basic macaron recipe, adding some brown colouring to achieve a good toffee colour.

* For the filling, place the chopped dates in a pan with the butter, rum, spices, syrup (or brown sugar) and vanilla extract and just cover with a little water. Cook gently, stirring occasionally for about 10 minutes until the liquids are absorbed.

* Stir in the cream and mix well. Purée the mix in a blender or food processor and set aside to cool.

* Transfer to a piping bag, arrange the macaron shells in pairs, pipe filling onto one shell of each pair and assemble.

* Leave in the fridge for at least 24 hours before serving.

*US fluid ounces

Exotic Fruit Macarons

MACARONS MANGUE ET FRUIT DE LA PASSION

150g organic egg whites
100g fine caster sugar
180g ground almonds
270g icing sugar
10g unsweetened cocoa powder *or*
Yellow and red colouring

100g organic butter, softened
10g cornflour
1 egg, beaten
120ml (4 fl oz*) liquidised mix of mango, passionfruit and pineapple (or a tropical fruit smoothie, already prepared)
The pulp of 2 passionfruits
To decorate: dessicated coconut, cocoa powder or edible metallic lustre

Enjoy with a cappuccino or latte coffee or serve with Yunnan, Earl Grey, Ceylon or Darjeeling teas. If serving at the end of a meal, they go well with fruity white wines such as Gewürztraminer or Riesling.

*US fluid ounces

If you are pressed for time or it's not the tropical fruit season, then you can cheat by using a tropical fruit "smoothie" from the chiller section of the supermarket. Tropical fruits go well with chocolate, so you could make some chocolate shells for duo-coloured macs.

To make **Tropical Fruits and Coconut Macarons**, make orange shells and sprinkle with dessicated coconut. For the pastry cream filling, why not add a little coconut flavouring or make with half coconut milk, half fruit juice (made up to 120ml) and a little extra sugar to taste.

* Make chocolate macarons using the basic macaron recipe, adding 10g unsweetened cocoa powder to the mix. If making duo-colour macarons, make half quantity chocolate as above and the other half a mixture of yellow with a dash of red.

* To make the filling, cream the butter and set aside.

* Whisk the cornflour and beaten egg.

* Heat the liquidised fruit (or the smoothie) and the pulp from the passionfruit then sieve out any passionfruit seeds. Add to the cornflour and egg mix, then put back on the heat, whisking continuously until creamy and thickened.

* Once cool, beat in the creamed butter. Transfer to a piping bag, arrange the macaron shells in pairs, pipe filling onto one shell of each pair and assemble.

* Leave in the fridge for at least 24 hours before serving. Finish off with a dusting of cocoa powder, bronze lustre or with dessicated coconut.

Macaron Presentation

THE MACARON DOME

For special occasions, why not make your own macaron centre display. Simply use a clean, dry bowl and turn it upside down. Melt a bar of dark cooking chocolate in a bowl over a pan of boiling water (*bain-marie*), then leave to cool for no longer than 10 minutes. Brush the chocolate onto the bowl using a pastry brush. Using a mixture of colourful macarons (or simply two different colours), dab a bit of melted chocolate onto the middle of each macaron in turn and stick it onto the chocolate dome. Continue all the way around the bowl, working quickly before the chocolate hardens.

Julie

Macaron Presentation

MACARON FLOWERS

Create your own flowerpot with macaron flowers. Simply stick green crèpe paper on BBQ wooden skewers and push into a base of Oasis block, children's modelling clay (or even gingerbread) in a flowerpot. Ensure that the macarons are kept out of the sun so that the ganache doesn't melt too quickly in the middle. You'll find, however, that the centrepiece doesn't last that long at parties, as the macarons are devoured at an impressive rate!

However, if you do decide to keep them as a decoration you will find that they do actually last for about a month (just make sure you don't eat them!) For special effect, you could rub metallic powdered colouring on the macaron shells.

MAD MACS

Macarons can sometimes be found with savoury fillings such as onion jam or tomato jelly, or with fish combinations or salty olives. To be totally honest, I find the sweet macaron and these kind of fillings too sickly and difficult to place before or during a meal.

My solution has been a challenge: to cut down on the sugar in the meringue as much as I dare without it affecting its appearance and to introduce naturally sweet combinations such as beetroot, tomato, and sweet herbs which are less shocking to the palate. But the ultimate has been the creation of macarons with hot spice – "hot macs".

The following macarons are rather different and can be a sensation with guests when served with drinks before dinner. Or surprise them even further as an *amuse-bouche* served before a starter with a mini dish of creamy soup or to garnish a brochette of prawns. The secret is to make them as small as you possibly can (you want your guests begging for more). You will find this easier if you use a smaller nozzle (6mm/¼") with the piping bag.

For the hot macs, don't be afraid to augment the spice to your own tastes – you will find that the more fiery heat there is in the macaron, the more strongly your "sweet" macaron sensation comes in to put out the fire. If you do freeze the spicy ones, don't freeze them for more than a couple of weeks, as the spice does diminish. *Bon appétit*!

Sweet Garden Herb Macarons

MACARONS AUX HERBES DU JARDIN

75g organic egg whites
40g fine caster sugar
90g ground almonds
125g icing sugar
Pinch of salt
Green colouring

Sprig each of fresh basil leaves and fresh mint leaves
3 tbsps olive oil
Few drops of aniseed cordial (unsweetened)

Serve with a light white, rosé or red with good acidity such as a Portuguese Vinho Verde, a French Provençal rosé or an Italian red Chianti.

These taste better in the summer when the herbs are freshest and most fragrant. Unlike the other macarons, you don't need to wait 24 hours before eating them.

* Follow the basic macaron recipe, adding a dash of green colouring and a pinch of salt. Pipe out the smallest light-green macarons that you can produce.

* Mix even amounts of fresh mint and basil leaves (the sweeter herbs work best, but you could also add some coriander and parsley) in a blender with a few drops of the aniseed cordial and some olive oil.

* Arrange the macaron shells in pairs, dribble filling onto one shell of each pair using a teaspoon, and assemble.

* Chill in the fridge for about 6 hours before serving.

Bloody Mary Macarons

MACARONS BLOODY MARY

75g organic egg whites
40g fine caster sugar
90g ground almonds
125g icing sugar
Good pinch of salt
Red colouring
Black colouring

Try this tomato macaron with a different kick to it and have fun with the garnishes. You could serve them on a frosted glass platter, garnished with a lime wedge and filled with crudités such as celery and carrot sticks.

For the mocktail version, simply replace the vodka with tomato juice.

50g organic butter, softened
½ tsp celery salt
5g cornflour
½ egg, beaten
50g vodka
2 tbsps tomato purée (tomato paste)*
1 tbsp Worcestershire sauce*
Zest of ½ untreated lime
1 tbsp Tabasco sauce

- Follow the basic macaron recipe, adding a good pinch of salt and a dash of red colouring. Pipe out the smallest red macarons that you can produce. Just before baking them in the oven, decorate them with paint-brush flicks of black colouring to look like Worcestershire sauce!
- For the filling, cream the butter and the celery salt. Set aside for now.
- Whisk the cornflour and beaten egg together in a bowl. Heat the vodka, tomato purée, Worcestershire sauce, lime zest and Tabasco in a saucepan. Add to the cornflour mix, then transfer back to the heat whisking constantly until creamy and thickened. Set aside to cool.
- Once cool, beat in the creamed butter to the mix, then transfer to a piping bag. Arrange the macaron shells in pairs, pipe filling onto one shell of each pair and assemble.
- Chill for at least 24 hours in the fridge before serving.

Serve with pre-dinner drinks such as chilled vodka or a dry Martini. They go well with a light and fruity Chenin Blanc, a light rosé or a chilled red from the Loire.

* If following a gluten-free diet check ingredients of these products. UK Worcestershire Sauce contains gluten, US Worcestershire Sauce does not.

Tikka Macsala

A HOT MAC!

75g organic egg whites
40g fine caster sugar
90g ground almonds
125g icing sugar
Caramel and yellow colouring
2g curry powder
Pinch of salt

50g organic butter, softened
1 tbsp chopped fresh coriander
1 tsp ground garam masala
Pinch of cayenne pepper
5g cornflour
½ egg, beaten
50g single cream
1 tbsp tikka masala curry paste (or stronger if you like it hot!)*
¼ red chilli, diced very finely

I served this as an apéritif with a choice of a fruity white wine such as Gewürztraminer, Chenin Blanc (Saumur or Savennières also good from the Loire) lager or gin and tonic!

* If following a gluten-free diet check ingredients of this product

I'm so proud of this creation since even a discerning French chef thought it was sensational. I wanted to see if the classic "British" dish could be transformed into a macaron and now it's up to you to try it. You will become addicted, be warned! Adapt the quantity and strength of the curry paste according to your own taste. I personally think the more heat, the better, as the sweetness of the macaron shell puts out the fire. You have five seconds of the most original-tasting sensation! Also add the tiniest sliver of red chilli before putting on the tops. Dynamite!

Alternatively, impress your dinner guests by serving these hot macs with velvety velouté soups such as carrot, parsnip and coriander, creamy cauliflower, or Jerusalem artichoke.

* Follow the basic macaron recipe, adding a dash of caramel and yellow colouring at the meringue stage. Then, when sifting the ground almonds and icing sugar, add the curry powder and a pinch of salt. Pipe out the smallest macarons you can.

* For the filling, cream the butter, add the chopped coriander, garam masala, cayenne pepper and set aside. Whisk the cornflour and beaten egg together.

* Gently heat the milk with the curry paste then add to the cornflour and egg mix. Return to the heat, whisking constantly, until creamy and thickened. Set aside to cool.

* Once cool, beat in the spicy creamed butter. Transfer the mix to a disposable piping bag (the strong curry tends to linger on your washable bag). Arrange the macaron shells in pairs, pipe filling onto one shell of each pair. Assemble them adding a finely chopped red chilli fleck on the top of the cream

* Chill in the fridge for at least 24 hours before serving.

Beetroot and Horseradish Macarons

MACARONS BETTERAVE ET RAIFORT

75g organic egg whites
40g fine caster sugar
90g ground almonds
125g icing sugar
Pinch of salt
Red and blue colouring

50g organic butter, softened
5g cornflour
½ egg
50ml organic beetroot juice
1–1½ tbsps creamed horseradish*
25g cooked beetroot, finely grated or chopped
1 tbsp freshly grated horseradish (to garnish; or use a small amount of wasabi paste)

Serve with a glass of red Burgundy.

* If following a gluten-free diet check ingredients of this product

As a Scot (a native of colder climes) I just love the humble beetroot, so I transformed it into a macaron – and discovered by adding some spice that the "savoury" macaron didn't seem so strange after all! These were a winner when I served them as an apéritif at Christmas. As they're small, you pop them in your mouth in one go (the French use the verb *gober*, to swallow them whole!) They're also rather special added as a garnish to a beetroot and ginger risotto.

You'll see: you quickly get the heat from the horseradish and in the next second or two the sweet macaron puts out the fire! If you can't get a hold of fresh horseradish, add a dash of wasabi.

* Follow the basic macaron recipe, adding a good dash of red colouring with a hint of blue and a pinch of salt. Pipe out the smallest beetroot macarons that you can produce.

* For the filling, cream the butter and set aside.

* Whisk the cornflour and beaten egg together. Heat the beetroot juice, add to the cornflour mix, then transfer back to the heat, whisking constantly until thickened. Add the creamed horseradish according to taste and allow to cool.

* Once the mixture is cool, beat in the creamed butter. Transfer the mixture into a piping bag. Arrange the macaron shells in pairs, pipe filling onto one shell of each pair. Add the grated beetroot and a sliver of freshly grated horseradish on top of the creamy filling and assemble. (If you're using wasabi in place of the grated horseradish, add a tiny amount directly on the underside of the top shells before assembly.)

* Chill in the fridge for at least 24 hours before serving. I suggest that these are not frozen as the spice does diminish slightly after freezing.

Thai Green Curry Macarons

MACARONS AU CURRY VERT THAÏ

75g organic egg whites
40g fine caster sugar
90g ground almonds
125g icing sugar
Pinch of salt
Apple green colouring
1 tbsp black sesame seeds

50g organic salted butter, softened
2 tbsp fresh basil, finely chopped
Zest of 1 untreated lime, finely grated
5g cornflour
½ egg, beaten
50g coconut milk*
1 tbsp Thai green curry paste*

Serve as an apéritif with lager or fruity white wines such as Gewürztraminer, Riesling or Chenin Blanc.

After the Tikka Macsala macarons, I couldn't resist trying out a Thai curry version.

The recipe uses a green curry paste but you can easily adapt it to your own taste, perhaps using a red curry paste and altering the colouring of the macaron shells to vibrant red! Better still, make a duo-colour macaron of green and bright chilli red.

Alternatively, impress your dinner guests by serving these along with a starter such as flash-fried scallops or tiger prawns with a Thai-style sauce and garnish with a lime wedge.

A macaron to Thai for (sorry!).

* Follow the basic macaron recipe, adding a good dash of green colouring and a pinch of salt. Pipe out the smallest green macarons that you can produce. At *croûter* stage sprinkle them with black sesame seeds for a touch of the exotic.

* For the filling, cream the butter, add the chopped basil and lime zest and set aside. Whisk the cornflour and beaten egg together.

* Gently heat the coconut milk with the curry paste. Then add to the cornflour and egg mix. Return to the heat, whisking constantly until creamy and thickened. Cover the mixture with clingfilm and set aside to cool.

* Once cool, beat in the creamed butter with the basil and lime. Transfer the mix to a disposable piping bag (the curry flavours are strong and may linger for future macaron flavours). Arrange the macaron shells in pairs, pipe filling onto one shell of each pair and assemble.

* Chill in the fridge for at least 24 hours before serving.

* If following a gluten-free diet check ingredients of these products

DAZZLING MACARON DESSERTS

You just *have* to show these off to your guests! They are a spectacular end to a meal. Without much effort, you can produce these giant macarons topped with light perfumed cream and seasonal fruits, which looks like you've produced something terribly chic straight from a Parisian pâtisserie.

These are made with large macaron shells. They are quicker to prepare than the macarons in the previous chapters as they are open, so no need to wait 24 hours for any filling to settle. The macaron bases can be made in advance or frozen until required. I like to make more than I need and freeze the rest so that if impromptu guests arrive, or when I don't have much time in the kitchen, I can rely on my macaron bases and produce a stunning dessert in no time (just remember to keep a stock of mascarpone).

If, however, you don't have any leftovers, then you can use 50g egg whites, 33g caster sugar, 60g ground almonds, 90g icing sugar which is enough to make six giant macarons with a 6–7cm (2") diameter.

Simply prepare the cream and dress them a couple of hours before serving. Even easier, if pressed for time, just dollop on a large scoop of ice cream or sorbet on top at the last minute.

The following recipes are for six servings. All of these desserts go beautifully with an off-dry or demi-sec Champagne.

Rose Macaron with Rose and Raspberry Cream

MACARON GÉANT ROSE-FRAMBOISES

6 large rose macarons*:
50g egg whites
33g caster sugar
60g ground almonds
90g icing sugar
Red colouring
(* Or retrieve the macaron bases from your stock in the freezer)

600g raspberries
2 tbsps caster sugar
3 tbsps rosewater
Few drops of rose extract
250g tub of mascarpone

Serve with an off-dry or pink Champagne, or a fruity Gewürztraminer (vendanges tardives).

This is a classic in most fabulous French pâtisseries, although this is a much quicker version that you can make at home with mascarpone. It's divine! Alternatively you could make giant pistachio macarons as your base but still flavour the cream with rosewater (please see my note about rosewater on page 45).

For Valentine's Day or an anniversary, you could pipe out giant love heart shapes as the base and decorate with rose petals.

* Using the basic recipe, prepare 6 large rose macarons, using a few drops of red colouring. When using the piping bag, start working your way out from the middle in a spiral shape to form a larger circle about 6–7cm (2") in diameter. Baking time will be between 10–15 minutes, depending on your oven. (Or retrieve the macaron bases from your stock in the freezer.)

* For the cream: mash 12 raspberries with the sugar, rosewater, rose extract and mascarpone. Whisk together until light and fluffy. Serve on top of each giant rose macaron and place plenty of fresh raspberries on top.

* To serve, dust lightly with icing sugar and decorate with fresh rose petals. For special occasions, whisk in the pulp of a passion fruit and decorate with green marzipan leaf shapes or pink marzipan rose shapes (see Stockists, page 127).

* Chill for about 1 hour before serving.

Pistachio Macaron with Strawberries and Cream

MACARON GÉANT PISTACHES-FRAISES

6 large pistachio macarons*:
50g egg whites
33g caster sugar
60g ground almonds
90g icing sugar
Green colouring
(* Or retrieve the macaron bases from your stock in the freezer)

600g strawberries
2 tbsp caster sugar
1 tsp almond extract
2 tbsps ground pistachios
250g tub of mascarpone

Serve with a demi-sec or pink Champagne, sparkling Vouvray wine from the Loire or Moscato d'Asti.

This great-looking dessert is also beautiful with wild strawberries if you can find them.

Dust lightly with icing sugar and decorate with freshly ground pistachios and a basil top or mint leaves. Alternatively top with one shell of a medium-sized pistachio macaron.

* Using the basic recipe, prepare 6 large pistachio macarons. When using the piping bag, start working your way out from the middle in a spiral shape to form a larger circle about 6–7cm (2") in diameter. Baking time will be between 10–15 minutes, depending on your oven.

* Mash 3 strawberries with the sugar, almond extract, 1 tbsp ground pistachios and the mascarpone. Whisk together until light and fluffy. Serve on top of a giant macaron and place plenty of fresh halved strawberries on top, or leave them whole if they are smaller woodland strawberries.

* Sprinkle the remaining ground pistachios over the top of each dessert.

* Chill for about 1 hour before serving.

Caramel Macaron "Tatin"-style

MACARON GÉANT FAÇON TATIN

6 large caramel macarons*:
50g egg whites
33g caster sugar
60g ground almonds
90g icing sugar
Caramel colouring
(* Or retrieve the macaron bases from your stock in the freezer)

4 granny smith apples, peeled, cored and sliced
25g unsalted butter
3 tbsps sugar
½ tsp ground cinnamon
6 tbsps caramel/butterscotch sauce
Vanilla or caramel ice cream
Ground cinnamon or metallic powdered colouring to decorate

Serve with a dessert wine such as Rivesaltes Ambré, an Alsace Riesling (late harvest) or a tawny port.

This is another simple but scrumptious dessert inspired by the *Tarte-Tatin*, which is an upside-down caramelised apple tart.

* Using the basic recipe, prepare 6 large caramel macarons. When using the piping bag, start working your way out from the middle in a spiral shape to form a larger circle about 6–7cm (2") in diameter. Baking time will be between 10–15 minutes, depending on your oven.
* Sauté the apple slices in a non-stick frying pan with the butter and sugar until the apples are golden and translucent. Sprinkle them with the cinnamon.
* Serve on top of each giant caramel macaron with a dollop of ice-cream and dribble over some caramel sauce on each.
* To garnish, dust the plate with more ground cinnamon or with some bronze metallic colouring.

Chocolate Macaron with Mango and Passionfruit

MACARON GÉANT CHOCOLAT, MANGUE ET FRUIT DE LA PASSION

6 large chocolate macarons*:
50g egg whites
33g caster sugar
60g ground almonds
90g icing sugar
4g unsweetened cocoa powder
Brown food colouring
(* Or retrieve the macaron bases from your stock in the freezer)

Half a ripe mango
3 passionfruits
2 tbsps caster sugar
250g mascarpone
Cocoa powder or grated coconut to decorate

Serve with a late harvest Gewürztraminer or other dessert wines such as Rivesaltes, Banyuls, Maury or Rasteau.

As well as flavouring the cream with passionfruit, reserving the juice and pulp of one passionfruit to garnish this dish is an attractive and mouth-watering addition.

* Using the basic recipe, prepare 6 large chocolate macarons. When using the piping bag, start working your way out from the middle in a spiral shape to form a larger circle about 6–7cm (2") in diameter. Baking time will be between 10–15 minutes, depending on your oven.

* For the cream, mash the mango and sieved pulp of 2 passionfruits with the sugar and mascarpone. Whisk together until light and fluffy.

* Serve on top of each giant chocolate macaron and dribble the pulp from the last passionfruit over it.

* To garnish, dust the plate with dark cocoa powder and grated coconut. You could also add fine slivers of the other half of the mango.

* Chill for about 1 hour before serving.

Coffee Macaron with Tiramisu Cream

MACARON GÉANT TIRAMISU

6 large coffee macarons*:
50g egg whites
33g caster sugar
60g ground almonds
90g icing sugar
1 tsp coffee granules
(* Or retrieve the macaron bases from your stock in the freezer)

2 tbsps strong espresso coffee
2 eggs, separated
3 tbsps caster sugar
250g mascarpone
1 tsp bitter almond extract
250g raspberries (optional)
To decorate: toasted pecan nuts, cocoa powder or chocolate coffee beans

Serve with a tawny port, sweet sherry or a dessert wine such as Muscat. Also delicious with some Amaretto liqueur.

This dessert also works just as well with giant chocolate macaron bases. These go beautifully with roasted figs in Marsala.

* Prepare 6 large coffee macarons using the basic recipe, and adding 1 tsp coffee granules to the mix before baking. When using the piping bag, start working your way out from the middle in a spiral shape to form a larger circle about 6–7cm (2") in diameter. Baking time will be between 10–15 minutes, depending on your oven.

* Prepare some strong coffee and leave it to cool.

* For the cream, whisk the two egg whites with the caster sugar until the whites form stiff peaks. In a bowl, mix together the mascarpone with the egg yolks until smooth.

* Add 2 tbsps of the cooled coffee and the almond extract to the mascarpone mix and gently fold in the egg whites.

* Spoon on top of each giant macaron base and, if using, place the raspberries on top. If fresh raspberries aren't available then decorate with toasted pecan nuts. Refrigerate until needed.

* When ready to serve, dust with unsweetened cocoa powder and decorate with chocolate coffee beans.

* Chill for about 1 hour before serving.

Sticky Toffee Macaron Pudding

MACARON GÉANT "STICKY TOFFEE PUDDING"

6 large toffee-coloured macarons*:
50g egg whites
33g caster sugar
60g ground almonds
90g icing sugar
Caramel/brown colouring
(* Or retrieve the macaron bases from your stock in the freezer)

400g soft medjool dates, pitted and chopped
50g unsalted organic butter
3 tbsp dark rum
½ tsp mixed spice powder
Few drops of vanilla extract

Toffee sauce:
85g dark brown sugar (muscovado)
150ml (5 fl oz**) double cream
100g unsalted butter
2 tbsps golden syrup

Serve with a late harvest Riesling or other dessert wines such as a Rivesaltes Ambré or Monbazillac.

**US fluid ounces

No dessert chapter could be complete without our favourite sticky toffee pudding! I can't say this is necessarily a lighter version of the British classic but at least it's gluten free and just as wickedly sticky.

* Using the basic recipe, prepare 6 large toffee-coloured macarons, using brown colouring. When using the piping bag, start working your way out from the middle in a spiral shape to form a larger circle about 6–7cm (2") in diameter. Baking time will be between 10–15 minutes, depending on your oven.

* For the sticky date topping, place the chopped dates in a pan with the butter, rum, spices and vanilla extract and just cover with a little water. Cook gently, stirring occasionally for about 10 minutes until the liquids are absorbed. Set aside.

* Prepare the sauce. Gently melt all the ingredients in a saucepan on a low heat for 5 minutes until the sauce is smooth, then bring the sauce to the boil (still on quite a low heat) to thicken it nicely.

  (For busy gourmets, you can buy ready-made sticky toffee pudding sauce.)

* Serve the sticky date mixture on top of each macaron base and dribble over the warm toffee sauce directly at the table. You could also serve this with some ice cream for a totally decadent finish.

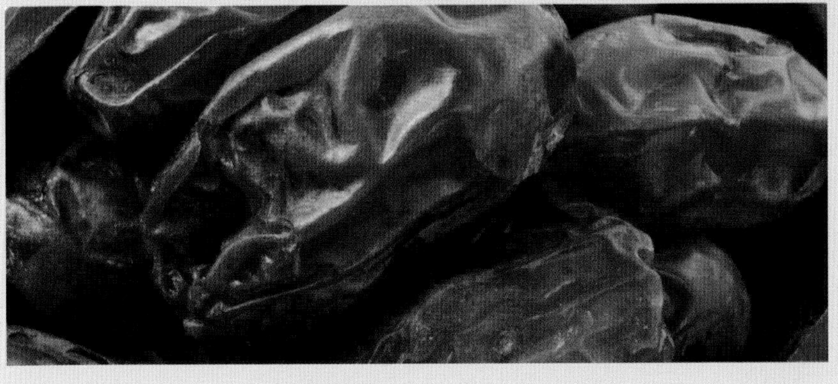

APPENDIX:

WHAT TO DO WITH YOUR EGG YOLKS ... AND MORE

Storing egg whites in the fridge for your macarons is all very well, but what can you make to use up your egg yolks? Whilst egg whites can keep in the fridge for up to a week (you can also freeze egg whites), fresh egg yolks need to be consumed quickly. So for us thrifty gourmets who don't want to waste good yolks – which are an excellent source of protein, vitamin B, vitamin A, D and E, zinc and iron – here are some ideas for using them up.

Although space doesn't allow us to include recipes for all of them here, on the following pages you'll find a list of ideas for what to do with extra egg yolks and many of the recipes for these can be found in the Bonus Recipes section of my website MadAboutMacarons.com.

On the following pages you'll find my recipes for mayonnaise, crème brulée and vanilla ice cream.

Recipe Ideas for Egg Yolks

Crème Brulée: See recipe on page 124.
Pots de Crème: Just like the crème brulée, but it's without the crunchy "burnt" topping. Includes crème catalane.
Chocolate Cake: Add an egg yolk to a chocolate cake to make it richer and more gooey (more like a fondant). This also works for chocolate brownies.
Custard: Uses 4 yolks.
Crème Anglaise: Custard sauce, or *crème anglaise*, uses 4 yolks for this classic sauce served mainly with chocolate desserts.
Chocolate Mousse: White or dark chocolate mousse, coffee mousse, fruit mousse.
French Toast: Add an extra yolk to one beaten egg, milk, sugar and vanilla for a speedy top-notch dessert to use up old bread, brioche or even scones.
Ice cream: Home-made always tastes better! See page 125 for the recipe.
Glazing: On top of pastries, bread, brioches for that enticing golden crust.
Lemon Curd: Uses 4–5 egg yolks.
Quiches and Tarts: Simply add an extra egg yolk to your basic egg-and-cream mix for savoury or sweet tarts or tartelettes.
Pasteis de Nata: Use 6 yolks for this Portuguese classic puff-pastry custard tart.
Sabayon or **Zabaglione**: Uses 6 yolks with sugar and Marsala wine.
Rice Pudding: Add an extra luxury to your rice pudding. Beat together 2 yolks with 2 tbsps of caster sugar until light and creamy. Then beat into the cooked rice pudding.
Mayonnaise: See page opposite for recipe.
Béarnaise or **Hollandaise Sauces**: Both require 3 yolks.
Greek Béchamel Sauce for Moussaka: Add 2 yolks to normal béchamel sauce to top moussaka. This will ensure your topping will have a light glaze.
Blanquette de Veau (veal casserole): Add 2 yolks at the end of cooking to thicken the sauce.
Creamy Lemon Sauce for Pasta: Mix 2 egg yolks, a small tub of crème fraîche, the zest and juice from an untreated lemon, some freshly grated parmesan, poppy seeds, finely chopped parsley and season. Add to cooked spaghetti at the end of cooking for a speedy pasta dish with prawns.

Mayonnaise

THE CLASSIC DRESSING

2 egg yolks
½ tsp sea salt
1–2 tsp Dijon mustard
200ml (6.5 fl oz*) olive oil
1 tbsp white wine vinegar (plain or herbal)

Preparation time: 10–15 minutes

Ensure that your ingredients are at room temperature to make the perfect mayo.

There are all sorts of variations you can make with mayonnaise: for a herby mayo, add lemon or lime juice and zest and some freshly chopped herbs; crush 4 garlic cloves with a teaspoon of sea salt and you have the perfect *Aïoli*; add 1–2 tsps of wasabi for an extra kick to serve with seafood and fishcakes; and to make a classic tartare sauce, simply add a tablespoon each of finely chopped gherkins, capers, dill, parsley and the juice of ½ lemon (see picture below).

* Whisk the egg yolks, salt and mustard with a metallic whisk in a glass bowl. Gradually add the olive oil, dribbling it finely and regularly, whisking all the time. Once the mixture starts to thicken, add the white wine vinegar (I have a lovely tarragon vinegar which works nicely).

* The mayonnaise can keep for three days in an airtight jar in the fridge.

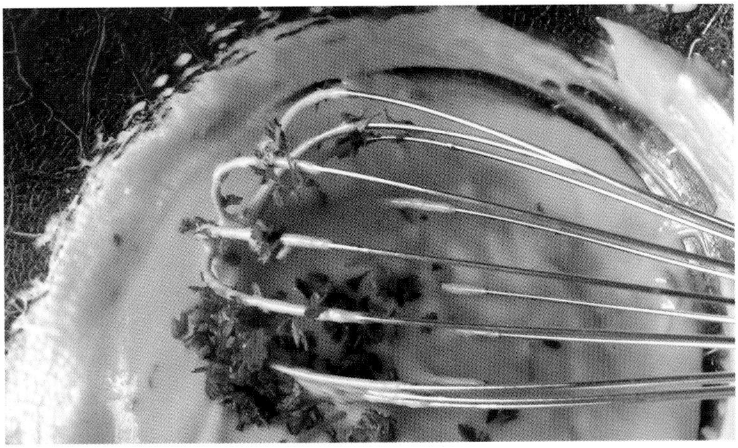

*US fluid ounces

Crème Brulée

CRACKLING CREAMS

8 egg yolks
80g caster sugar
600ml cream [1 1/3 US pint] (or 400ml [13.5 fl oz*] cream/200ml [6.7 fl oz*] whole milk)
1 vanilla pod
4 tbsps Demerara sugar for caramelising

(See picture on page 120.) Serve mini versions in funky little yoghurt pots or shot glasses and serve with a macaron on top! (See picture below.)

Variations: it's so easy to make up your own variations, as you can infuse all sorts of flavours in the cream, such as pistachio, lemon, orange, lavender, Earl Grey tea, coffee. The French also love savoury crème brulée, such as with foie gras!

* Preheat oven to 120°C.

* Mix yolks and sugar until creamy. Heat the cream and vanilla pod in a pan until warm. Remove the vanilla pod and scrape out the seeds into the cream then pour over the egg mixture and mix thoroughly.

* Pour into individual ramekins and place in a *bain-marie* (a roasting tray filled halfway up with water will suffice) in the oven for about 1hour 15mins. Leave them to cool, then chill for 2 hours in the fridge.

* Before serving, dust with the demerara sugar then caramelise them quickly with a blowtorch or under a hot grill.

* You could also serve with the shell of a pistachio macaron on top.

*US fluid ounces

Vanilla Ice Cream

CRÈME GLACÉE À LA VANILLE

8 egg yolks
120g caster sugar
400ml (13.5 fl oz*) whole milk
200ml (6.7 fl oz*) whipping cream
1 vanilla pod

Ideally, it's best to have an ice cream machine. If you don't have one, then just take the cream out of the freezer every 30 minutes (about 5 times) and mix up the partially frozen mixture well.

Home-made always tastes better and the beauty is that you can vary the flavours, too. For example, simply replace the vanilla pod with the grated zests of 2 lemons for lemon ice-cream; 3 tablespoons of coffee powder for coffee ice-cream; 2 tbsps finely chopped mint; 2 tablespoons macha green tea; toasted walnuts and toffee. The list is endless.

Needless to say, decorate with a macaron or decorate a macaron with the ice cream!

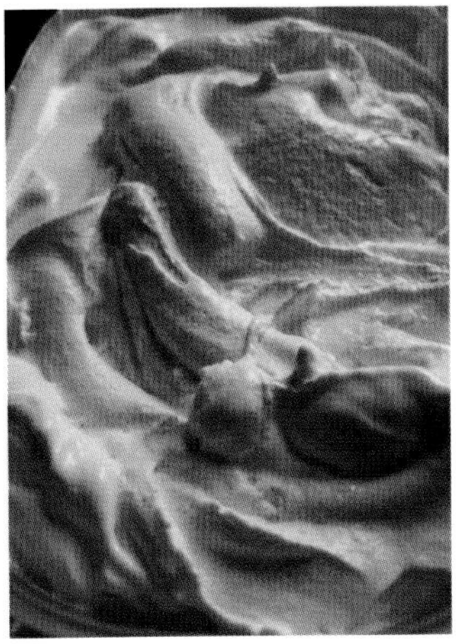

* Cream together the egg yolks and sugar in a large bowl until light and creamy.

* Heat the milk and cream in a heavy-based pan with the vanilla pod, cut in two lengthways. Bring to the boil, then turn off the heat for the vanilla to infuse in the creamy milk for 5–10 minutes. Scrape out the seeds from the pod and add to the cream.

* Bring the creamy milk to the boil again and pour onto the egg mixture, whisking continuously. Return the mixture to the pan on a medium heat, whisking constantly until the custard thickens and coats the back of a spoon. Remove the vanilla pod and set the mixture aside to cool.

* Once cool, place in the fridge for 1–2 hours before pouring into an ice cream machine to churn.

*US fluid ounces

Quick Reference Guide for Egg Whites

As you can't always predict the exact amount of egg whites you have saved up in advance, here are some conversions. Stick it on your fridge for quick reference. One egg white is about 35g. When making smaller quantities of macarons it is easier to make a chocolate ganache for them.

150g egg whites
100g caster sugar
180g ground almonds
270g icing sugar

140g egg whites
92g caster sugar
168g ground almonds
252g icing sugar

130g egg whites
86g caster sugar
156g ground almonds
234g icing sugar

120g egg whites
79g caster sugar
144g ground almonds
216g icing sugar

110g egg whites
72g caster sugar
132g ground almonds
198g icing sugar

100g egg whites
66g caster sugar
120g ground almonds
180g icing sugar

75g egg whites
50g caster sugar
90g ground almonds
135g icing sugar

60g egg whites
40g caster sugar
72g ground almonds
108g icing sugar

50g egg whites
33g caster sugar
60g ground almonds
90g icing sugar

Savoury (reduced sugar):
75g egg whites
40g caster sugar
90g ground almonds
125g icing sugar

50g egg whites
30g caster sugar
60g ground almonds
80g icing sugar

Stockists

Flavourings and Extracts

UK
willieschocolateshop.com
thecakedecoratingcompany.co.uk
goodnessdirect.co.uk
spicesofindia.co.uk
steenbergs.co.uk
vanillabazaar.com
funkyraw.com
healthysupplies.co.uk
squires-shop.com

US
lorannoils.com
jrmushroomsandspecialties.com
pastrychef.com
cacao-barry.com
wilton.com

Colouring, Edible Lustres

UK
cakecraftshop.co.uk
almondart.com
cakescookiesandcraftsshop.co.uk
gold-gourmet.com

US
uscakesupply.com
pastrychef.com
wilton.com

Garnishes, Cutters, Moulds, Stencils

UK
thecakedecoratingcompany.co.uk
almondart.com
cakecraftshop.co.uk
lindyscakes.co.uk

US
wilton.com

Almonds, Fillings, and UK brands

US
igourmet.com
teaandsympathynewyork.com
kalustyans.com
americanalmond.com
nutsonline.com
earthfare.com
thefreshmarket.com

Cake Boxes and Gift Bags

UK
bagnboxman.co.uk
cakeboxesdirect.com
littleboxcompany.com
diyfavourboxes.co.uk
thefavourboxshop.co.uk

US
wilton.com
brpboxshop.com

French Brands

UK
mondizen.com
frenchclick.co.uk
marketquarter.com
thegoodfoodnetwork.co.uk
macknade.com

US
thefrenchybee.com
saveurdujour.com
igourmet.com

American Terms

UK TERM		US TERM
baking sheet	–	cookie sheet, sheet pan
beetroot	–	beet
bicarbonate of soda	–	baking soda
bitter almond extract	–	almond extract/essence. All almond extract and essence is made from bitter almonds whether it is labelled "bitter" or not
caster (or castor) sugar	–	superfine sugar
clingfilm	–	Saran wrap/plastic wrap
coriander	–	cilantro
cornflour	–	cornstarch (the thickening agent, a white powder)
custard powder (Birds)	–	main ingredients are cornflour/cornstarch and vanilla flavouring. If you can't find any, just use cornstarch and vanilla extract. Some other flan powders may be a substitute but Birds is gluten free, other brands may not be.
demerara sugar	–	raw or turbinado sugar
dessicated coconut	–	flaked coconut
double cream	–	heavy cream (48% butterfat)
glacé	–	candied
fan oven	–	convection oven
Golden Syrup (Tate & Lyle)	–	nearest equivalent in consistency is corn syrup. Depending on recipe, for a closer taste to golden syrup than corn syrup provides, you could maybe substitute light-brown sugar.
greaseproof paper	–	baking parchment
ground almonds	–	almond flour
icing sugar	–	powdered, 10X, or confectioner's sugar
muscovado sugar	–	dark brown sugar
rosewater	–	some brands labelled rosewater are in fact essence. My rose macarons require rosewater made from water with added essence no more than about 6%. Use stronger rosewaters accordingly in smaller amounts than recipes state.
single cream	–	light cream
smoothie	–	blended/liquidised fresh fruit drink (not frozen)
tomato purée	–	tomato paste
unsalted butter	–	don't assume butter labelled "sweet butter" is unsalted. Check the ingredients list on the packaging. Also, only use 100% butter, not whipped butter or low-fat spreads.
whipping cream (only one kind in UK)	–	light whipping cream (30–36% butterfat), heavy whipping cream (36 – 40% butterfat). Choose light whipping cream where whipping cream is indicated in these recipes.
whisk (verb)	–	beat, whip
whole milk	–	full-fat (full-cream) milk, not skimmed or semi-skimmed milk. UK and US whole milk has the same butterfat content.

Troubleshooting

MERINGUE WON'T STIFFEN PROPERLY

Mixing bowl or beaters may have been dirty or oily

Ensure equipment is clean.

Yolk may have got into egg whites

Try easier method of egg separation (see Egg Tips, page 25).

Colour/essence added before whites reach stiff peaks

Don't add additional flavourings/colour until meringue stiff.

Eggs were too fresh or too cold, or egg whites not aged

Use eggs within their use-by date, but not the very freshest ones. Age whites in a covered jar in the fridge for four days. Use at room temperature.

BATTER TOO WET OR RUNNY

Too much additional flavouring, colour, or other liquid

Use powdered or paste colours and go easy on the flavourings.

Too much macaronnage/mixing

Mix batter until it falls like a ribbon.

Egg whites weren't beaten long enough

Beat egg whites until mixture reaches stiff, glossy peaks.

Beaten egg whites sat for too long unmixed

Prepare all your ingredients before you start. Work quickly.

Incorrect measurement of ingredients

Go back to the basic recipe and follow it to the letter.

MACARONS HAVE POINTED OR LUMPY SHELLS

Ground almonds were too rough/not ground enough

Sieve ground almonds and remove largest bits.

After piping there are points on macs that do not smooth out

Not enough mixing or too much icing sugar/ground almonds to meringue. To save the macarons, give the tray a rap or two on your work surface before they set, to see if that smoothes them out (this is the only reason for ever rapping the baking sheet).

MACARONS HAVE GREASY SPOTS ON SURFACE

Too much macaronnage

Stop mixing when ribbon stage is reached.

Too much grinding (e.g. if making own nut flour)

Mix some icing sugar with the nuts you are grinding.

MACARONS RUN INTO EACH OTHER

Batter too runny

See above.

Macarons were piped too big or too closely together

Leave more room between piped macarons.

MACARONS CRACK

Batter was too runny

See above. Runny batter creates a weak macaron shell.

Batter undermixed

Mix till it falls like a ribbon, and press out the bubbles.

Macarons did not croute/air long enough

Air for 30–60 mins. Humid room might necessitate longer airing.

Inconsistent airflow/too much humidity in oven

Too many trays in oven causes this. One at a time please.

NO PIEDS/FEET DEVELOP

Batter too runny

See above.

Insufficient crouting/airing

Allow to air for 30 minutes to an hour.

Cooked at too low a temperature

Use an oven thermometer to check your oven.

MACARONS STICK TO BAKING PARCHMENT

Not cooked long enough

Test one macaron in batch and continue baking if base is sticky.

Not left to cool before removal from sheet/pan

Leave them to cool on the warm-from-the-oven baking sheet.

MACARONS INCONSISTENT WITHIN ONE BATCH

Uneven airflow in your oven

Bake only one tray at a time. Verify oven temp with thermometer.

Meringue/colouring not incorporated properly

An unmixed streak of meringue or colour has weakened mixture.

MACARONS HOLLOW

Removed from heat before fully baking

Test one macaron in your batch. If base is sticky, bake longer.

Too many air bubbles in mixture

Press out air in batter with patisserie scraper. Don't fold.

MACARONS ARE TOO SOFT/SOGGY THE NEXT DAY

Shells not cooked enough

Test one in your batch and ensure bottom is dry and smooth.

Too much filling

Moisture from filling has dampened the macs too much.

Filling has too much liquid/fruit juice/alcohol in it

Ensure correct ratio of fruit pulp, etc., to butter.

Temperature changes

Avoid taking them from one temperature extreme to another.